"Starting with the fundamental stages of starting and building an idea into a business, Sally Frank has written the definitive textbook for healthcare innovators and entrepreneurs. Chapter by chapter, *The Startup Protocol* begins with the simple, then delineates and exemplifies the details. Even successful entrepreneurs who have designed and built multiple companies need a blueprint, and *The Startup Protocol* is the best I have seen in my nearly thirty years as an entrepreneur. Read it, study it, and dramatically improve your odds of success."

Michael Gorton, BS MS JD, Teladoc / Recuro Founder, 14x Serial Entrepreneur

"Sally is a true unicorn – a corporate executive who both cares about and understands the challenges of entrepreneurship, focusing on healthcare which is in desperate need of true innovation. This book is a reflection of that combination – providing a clear road-map and tools that address the tactical hurdles to success, as well as highlighting how to approach the existential challenges of starting and growing a company in a highly challenging environment."

Steve Tremitiere, Founder & CEO StraightLine Health

"This is an amazing body of work – super comprehensive and makes very nuanced and complicated topics very accessible. The book has extraordinary range, covering all the key topics."

Michael Greeley, General Partner, Flare Capital

"The author has done a spectacular job synthesizing complex information into a digestible format. She uses concrete examples to illustrate her points beautifully. This book was better than a year of business school. A must-read for any entrepreneur!"

Ranya Habash, MD, Co-founder of MetaMed, FDA Digital Health Network of Experts

"As an emergency physician, it is frustrating to see so many brilliant, passionate, and well-intended founders and entrepreneurs create so many products and solutions that have very little value in my real world of caring for patients. Sally has laid out a clear framework with actionable guidance for how to create truly world-changing solutions to the many crises we face daily in healthcare. If you want to leave a ripple in healthcare, reading *The Startup Protocol* is an excellent place to start."

Joshua Tamayo-Sarver, MD, PhD, FACEP, FAMIA, VP of Innovation at Vituity and Inflect Health

"Sally Frank's startup manual should be required reading for all new (and perhaps some seasoned) entrepreneurs who wish to build companies in digital health. The narrative is complete, easy to understand and chock full of links and references for those who wish to dig deeper. I can think of so many founders I've met over the years who would have benefited from this outstanding book."

Joseph Kvedar, MD, Professor, Harvard Medical School

"If you're a startup in the healthcare space this book is better than getting an MBA. Sally Frank does a masterful job of condensing years of real-world experience into instantly applicable knowledge, behaviors, and tools to help readers successfully navigate the complexities faced by any startup trying to make its way in the worlds of health and medicine."

Tom Lawry, Bestselling Author of "Hacking Healthcare," Global AI Transformation Advisor, and Former Startup Founder

"Sally delivers a unique perspective on successful digital health startups. Illuminating and inspiring for entrepreneurs looking to solve problems regardless of the industry. Excited to share the book's wisdom with the global entrepreneurs I mentor."

Patty Obermaier, Emerging Growth Officer, Microsoft Health and Life Sciences and Board Member of Global Good Fund

"Sally pulls on her extensive background in evaluating and growing health tech startups to create a comprehensive how-to guide on starting a company. The advice is well-organized, simple, and digestible and, most importantly, highly effective. I recommend this book for any health tech startup founder who wants to understand the end-to-end journey of getting a company off the ground."

Hans Yang, General Manager, Microsoft for Startups

The Startup Protocol

There are lots of founders and lots of ideas floating around to help improve the delivery of healthcare services and positively affect the health of each of us as individuals, as well as groups of patients afflicted by chronic or acute diseases. Unfortunately, many of these ideas never reach their full potential to improve patient outcomes or reduce costs of care. Sometimes, it's because the idea isn't feasible or scalable. Sometimes, it's because the market isn't ready, or regulators aren't ready. And sometimes, it's just because the founder or founding team has a blind spot (or two). Not only do these hidden blind spots ensure their failure, but in many cases, with better planning or a greater, more holistic understanding of the market forces, the blind spot can be overcome. Or better yet, the founder can realize that their idea is doomed from the start and consider other, better options to solve the problem they are attacking.

The goal of this book is to help founders and their teams identify blind spots and avoid the most common pitfalls of starting a digital health company. Having spent time with founders, VC companies, and most importantly, prospective digital health startups, patterns have emerged regarding those startups that are successful and those that die an often slow and painful death. While not a recipe for guaranteed success, having a guidebook of sorts can help navigate the perils associated with building a digital health company and can very likely improve the odds of success.

The book will go through the typical life cycle of an early-stage company, from ideation to the first few customer deals, and highlight best practices for tackling the challenges at each stage including:

- What problem are you trying to solve?
- And why are you trying to solve this problem?
- Who will help you build the solution and company?
- How will you build the solution?
- How will you pitch your company?
- How will you sell your solution?
- And, what does success look like to you, your stakeholders, and your customers?

The Startup Protocol

A Guide for Digital Health Startups to Bypass Pitfalls and Adopt Strategies That Work

Sally Ann Frank

Routledge
Taylor & Francis Group

A PRODUCTIVITY PRESS BOOK

Cover and chapter maps designed by: Ariadna Duran

First published 2024
by Routledge
605 Third Avenue, New York, NY 10158

and by Routledge
4 Park Square, Milton Park, Abingdon, Oxon, OX14 4RN

Routledge is an imprint of the Taylor & Francis Group, an informa business

© 2024 Sally Ann Frank

The right of Sally Ann Frank to be identified as author of this work has been asserted by her in accordance with sections 77 and 78 of the Copyright, Designs and Patents Act 1988.

ISBN: 9781032639451 (hbk)
ISBN: 9781032639444 (pbk)
ISBN: 9781032639468 (ebk)

DOI: 10.4324/9781032639468

Typeset in Garamond
by Deanta Global Publishing Services, Chennai, India

To all of the innovators, striving to improve our health and well-being.

Contents

Preface..xiii

Foreword xvii

Acknowledgments xix

About the Author xxi

1 The Problem 1
    Summary 8
    Resources...8
    Notes..8

2 The Solution..9
    Using Known Technology 11
    Using New(er) Technology 15
    The Business Model Gap..16
    Summary 17
    Resources...17
    Notes..17

3 The Regulations 19
    Data Privacy 21
    Medical Devices 23
        United States...24
        Europe and the UK...28
        UK..29
        Singapore..31
        Israel 31
    Change Management for Medical Devices 32
    Software 33
    Manufacturing and Good Practice (GxP) 34

Summary 35

Resources...35

Notes..35

4 The Technology..**37**

The Options 38

    AWS..39

    GCP..40

    Microsoft Azure 40

    Going Deeper..41

    Other Options 43

    Interoperability...45

    Reuse of Technology..47

Summary 47

Resources...47

Notes..48

5 The Funds **49**

Funding Basics 51

    Funding Types..52

Data Room 55

    Investor Pitch Deck..56

    Cap Table..66

    Historical P&L and Burn 67

    Making It Real 67

Summary 70

Resources...70

Notes..71

6 The Company **72**

The Company Structure...73

    The Team and Tribe...73

The Corporate Identity 80

    The Company Name 80

    The Logo 81

    The Mission Statement 82

    The Value Proposition..84

    The Tagline...86

    The Website..86

The Business Model 87
The Regulatory Journey 90
The Allure of Stealth 91
Summary 92
Resources 92
Notes 92

7 The Pitch 94
Personas 95
Titles 95
Roles 96
The Buying Process 96
The Deck 98
The Current Customers 99
The Offer 100
The Call to Action 102
The Caveats 103
Pitching to Win 106
Summary 107
Resources 107
Note 107

8 The Accelerators 109
The Accelerator Basics 110
The Right Accelerator for You 111
The Correct Fit 113
The Application 116
Summary 119
Resources 120
Notes 120

9 The GTM Strategies 121
Product-Market Fit 122
Confirming Product Market Fit 125
Proof of Concepts 128
Clinical Validation 128
Pilots 129
Land and Expand 129
Leverage Early Adopters 130

Validation to Production 133

Target Audience 135

Following Up 138

Social Media 139

Competition 140

Distribution 141

Managing the Pipeline 142

Summary 145

Resources 145

Notes 146

10 The Growth 149

Continual Learning 150

Continual Networking 152

Continual Evolution 155

This Is Just the Beginning 157

Summary 157

Resources 157

Notes 158

Index 159

Preface

In October of 2022, the Cedars Sinai Accelerator asked me to speak to their current cohort of digital health founders. Drawing from my experience, I started cataloging the common mistakes many founders make when trying to build a business. And while every startup is different, I had heard and seen the same blind spots across a variety of healthcare startups. This served as the foundation for my speech.

There is something unique about starting a company that is dedicated to helping people stay healthy, recover from illness, live with a chronic condition, or extend their lifespan. The founders behind health tech startups have an incredible sense of altruism and mission that is not replicated in the retail, financial, or other industries. Founders of those types of companies may have a mission, but nothing is as impactful and as important as healthcare and life sciences. Take Elizabeth O'Day for example. A Harvard PhD graduate and founder of Olaris, she has dedicated her life to improving how cancer patients receive treatment. Deeply affected by her brother's battle with cancer as a child, she witnessed what he went through during his treatments.[1] Even as a child, she felt compelled to do something to make cancer treatments personalized and less about trial and error. As a result, her company uses metabolomics to identify which treatment is best for each patient. Now, that's a mission worth pursuing! And Liz is not unique. Most of the digital health founders I've spoken to have a personal story that compelled them to push the boundaries of some aspect of healthcare delivery. These origin stories are heart-warming and sometimes heart-wrenching, and a tear or two is not out of the question (from me!). Whether the significant health event resulted in a good outcome or not, the mark in the founder's psyche has formed and the only thing that will help assuage their experience is trying to fix the system.

Necessity is the mother of all invention. Our population needs quality, accessible healthcare more than ever. Recent trends, including the aging of our population and the declining number of clinical professionals (either due to retirements or the great resignation), call into question our ability to manage the current care delivery models. Adding what we learned, tested, and adopted during the Covid-19 pandemic, which centered on telehealth, remote patient monitoring, and virtual clinical trials, the industry is not only ripe for disruption but it is desperately needed. Many of us believe technology is the answer to the question of improving healthcare delivery.

However, just as your doctor may have told you, "Moderation in all things." The same holds true for technology. The CIO of a major health system on the west coast shared with me that they have 3,000 applications deployed, 700 of which are designed for medical professionals. In reality, only 20–30 of those applications actually get used. His final comment to me was, "Turn that 20–30 into 15–18. That's what I need." That is what we all need. Simplicity, transparency, security, privacy, and efficiency are the hallmarks of the healthcare delivery system we all yearn for today.

But it's not just too much technology or too few staff that are concerning. We are struggling with access to care for many around the globe, and not just in the areas we typically consider underserved. Case in point, in a recent conversation with a physician in a major metropolitan area in the US, he shared that he was waiting 6 months for an appointment with a specialist in the same system *where he works.*

With that in mind, I am eager to have as many digital health startups succeed as possible, and if you are reading this book, you are, too. We need innovators and their innovations. We are at an inflection point where we either fix the system, or it breaks, and we all lose. All of us are familiar with the stories of organizations that did not see their demise because they became complacent. From buggy whips to Blockbuster, innovators were the ones pounding the nails into their commercial coffins. And let's not forget that the incoming physicians, PAs, and nurses are digital natives. We need them to be fulfilled by their work, which means judicious and effective use of technology. They won't stay in the profession long if they feel that antiquated systems and processes hamper them. Healthcare is much more than just a commercial enterprise. Our lives, dare I say, our social fabric, rely on just how we navigate the next few decades and how well we use technology as a force multiplier for our clinicians, scientists, and medical staff.

Before moving on, I want to outline a few semantic variations that will be used throughout this book. Digital health and health tech are meant to be synonymous and will be used interchangeably. Similarly, healthcare is used to denote providers and payers; while life sciences is used to denote pharma, medical devices, and biotechnology companies, unless otherwise stipulated. Lastly, clinicians are used in this book to identify anyone with a medical license, while staff refers to identify anyone in a support, non-clinical role. While some aspects of this book address characteristics of the global ecosystem, this book is designed primarily for startups in the United States or those eager to enter the US market.

Lastly and perhaps most importantly, this book is not designed to replace legal, financial, or commercial guidance. Nor will it guarantee success. It is also not a primer on how to write a killer business plan. There are plenty of books and courses on that subject (although, if you follow the steps in this book, you will be on your way to a comprehensive business plan). This book is designed to help you avoid making mistakes that I have seen derail digital health founders again and again. Armed with this knowledge, I hope that you can help us change and improve healthcare delivery. Let's ensure that you step over the potential pitfalls and get your solution to market faster, because we need it.

Before you dig into the rest of this book, it's probably a good time to outline the main stages in the life of a startup and how this book is organized. Though there are a variety of ways to convey the steps, here is how I break it down:

- **Ideate** – This is the stage where you have identified a problem, have an idea of how to solve it, and are considering building a business based on that idea. It may be something related to managing a chronic condition, accelerating drug discovery, or improving clinical workflows. You should be doing lots of research and vetting your idea with proxy customers.
- **Build** – In this phase, you are building your solution with the goal of building something you can present and test with proxy and prospective customers such as clinicians, scientists, and medical staff. This is also where you start building your business plan, minimally viable product (MVP). Additionally, you have begun the validation process, working with key clinical and scientific advisors.
- **Launch** – You have refined your MVP into a product, have completed initial validation, and are ready to introduce your product to the market, and are actively turning early adopters into paying customers while seeking out new customers. Your product complies with regulations, maintains patient privacy, and ensures data is secured.

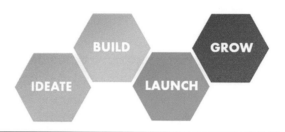

Figure 0.1   Steps in building a digital health startup.

Source: © Sally Ann Frank

■ **Grow** – You have a product you can sell and even a paying customer or two, having shown that you have achieved product-market-fit, i.e., the market is willing to buy your product at the price you set. At this stage, your product roadmap, regulatory pathway, and go-to-market strategy are aligned and integrated.

The remainder of this book is organized into these four stages (see Figure 0.1), although the lines between these stages are not hard and fast. Some chapters will fall into more than one stage, but due to the linear nature of reading (and writing), the concepts are presented in one stage only with references to other stages, when appropriate. Additionally, each chapter begins with a quote from a founder that I have spoken with at some point. I start with these quotes to convey what digital health startup founders may think and how to turn those sentiments into positive, productive steps toward launching a successful, sustainable digital health startup.

Note

1. Making space for the female founders of healthcare – Technology Record | The best of enterprise solutions from the Microsoft partner ecosystem.

Foreword

There are many reasons why this book is in the right place at the right time.

As generative AI becomes the headline of every pitch deck, it's challenging to separate the wheat from the chaff. What is the problem being solved? What is the product-market fit? Do I have to educate my customers as to why they need the solution or is that self-evident?

I receive dozens of pitch decks every week and 90% of them could be triaged away based on an incomplete "ideate" process. Do you really need your bathroom scale connected via Bluetooth to Twitter as part of a social network for weight loss? That's a solution in search of a problem.

As those of us in healthcare know, subtle variations in architecture and deployment strategy can make huge differences in implementation time. Privacy, security, compliance, IT, and legal all need to approve new healthcare applications that touch personally identified information or protected healthcare information. Requiring appliances behind the firewall or client device deployment of software can take 18 months just to get approved. The build should be cloud hosted, software as a service, clientless, and low impact on IT. These build decisions differentiate a growth company from a bankruptcy.

To me, the most important key performance indicator of any company is the adoption and actual use of their products. As the author notes in her preface, we don't need more niche point solutions used by a few people. We need platforms that reduce the number of applications to support and scale to a large number of users. Launching a product requires a careful analysis of user experience, operational maturity, and change management. It's very easy to get the launch wrong, no matter how good the product.

In today's marketplace, products cannot remain static. They must evolve and be responsive to market demands. They must be consistent and reliable to gain the trust of users. In the emerging world of AI products, there must be transparency – can we be sure AI models are fair, appropriate, valid, equitable, and safe? The area of scale and growth is where companies often falter. They start with 1 employee, grow to 10, reach 100, then plateau and stagnate. Often the innovator who did the ideation, build, and launch is not the right person to lead growth. Understanding the growth trajectory needed for companies to thrive and pre-determining the strategy saves countless discussions with board members and investors.

I was trained in emergency medicine, engineering, informatics, public policy, and company formation. I have no formal training as a startup CEO or company builder. In my youth, I thought I would personally need all the skills to start and run companies. Throughout my life, I've learned that surrounding yourself with great people and dividing up the work is the only way to scale. However, to be an effective leader you need to understand the strategy, structure, and staffing needed to move from ideation to growth. This book provides a roadmap for the entrepreneurial process so that you can quickly understand your knowledge gaps and assemble a team destined for success.

I wish I had this book when I started to lead innovation efforts. Its framework is timeless – technology will change, regulation will change, and cultural expectations will change, but the principles in this book will apply to whatever innovations come next.

John D. Halamka, MD

Acknowledgments

Writing is a very solitary endeavor; producing a book is anything but. I have so many people to thank for helping shuttle this work to the finish line. It's hard to know where to start, so I will give my thanks roughly in chronological order.

I must start with my parents, Mimi and Gordon Frank, for their ability to exemplify the value of hard work and continual learning. Special props to my Dad, posthumously, for suggesting I study computer science and business instead of fashion merchandising. Skipping ahead quite a bit, I want to thank Chris Lanier, who hired me into a role at Microsoft that uncovered a deep-seated, but unknown, passion for healthcare. I'd also like to thank Tom Davis for bringing me onto the Microsoft for Startup team and introducing me to the startup ecosystem, which ignited yet another passion.

This book would never have come into being without the counsel and guidance of my friend, Tom Lawry. Not only did he connect me to the terrific team at Taylor & Francis, led by amazing editor Kris Mednansky, but he encouraged me when the book was merely a whisper of a thought and continued to offer his guidance and support throughout the process. I have thoroughly enjoyed reading Tom's thought-provoking books on AI in healthcare and aspire to have the same impact on my readers.

I'm deeply grateful to John Halamka for writing the foreword to this book. An avid reader of his work, and follower of his thought leadership, having him review the early draft and respond with praise and willingness to introduce the book would have been unthinkable a few years ago. I clearly remember meeting him at the Connected Health Conference years ago in the green room before a session that I was to moderate, and he was one of the panelists. Although we had never met previously, John was kind and gracious, as we chatted for almost an hour prior to the session. We have continued our conversations about innovation, AI, and other topics, enabling me to continue to learn from his unique perspectives.

There were also several other people who read the unedited manuscript and provided invaluable feedback including Joe Kvedar, MD, Steve Tremitiere, Lisa Maki, Ranya Habash, MD, and Michael Greeley. Their recommendations were spot on and significantly improved the final version. My thanks also to Ariadna Duran, who designed the book's cover and the maps that guide these chapters.

Of course, behind the scenes are all the startup founders I've met and their willingness to share their hopes, dreams, and goals with me. These are the people who inspire me every day and I'm so very fortunate to be part of their tribe.

Lastly, I'd like to thank my husband, Scott Buchanan, for steadfastly encouraging me while putting up with my craziness as I wrote the book. He was the first to lay eyes on the manuscript, lovingly and painstakingly editing it before anyone else. With kindness and (oh so much) patience, Scott helps me keep things in perspective and like a serial founder, is always keen to find our next adventure.

Thank you all!

About the Author

**Sally Ann Frank** leads the worldwide Healthcare & Life Sciences (HLS) strategy, programs, and portfolio for Microsoft for Startups, an organization dedicated to accelerating the development of innovative companies. Through business strategy planning, go-to-market development, and technical excellence, she enables startups to achieve their revenue and long-term goals. Additionally, Sally directly mentors health and life sciences founders at all stages of their company's development to help them thrive and positively impact the global healthcare delivery system. She also works directly with enterprise companies, venture capitalists (VCs), accelerators, and other ecosystem players to facilitate connections, learning, and collaboration across the various stakeholders.

Previously, she was part of Microsoft's IoT Solutions team, helping healthcare and life sciences companies use internet of things (IoT) to improve patient outcomes and operational efficiency. With more than 25 years in the technology industry, she is focused on business outcomes, helping providers, payers, medical device, and pharmaceutical and life sciences companies use IoT, machine learning, AI, and a variety of other Microsoft technologies to meet the changing demands of the healthcare industry.

She earned an MBA from The George Washington University (Washington, DC), an MS in Systems Management from the University of Southern California, and a BS in Marketing with a minor in Computer Science from Virginia Tech.

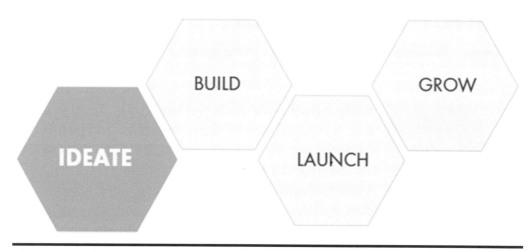

Figure 1.0 Ideate.

"Ideate" is a verb that means "to form an idea or conception of" or "to form ideas."[2,3] It comes from the medieval Latin word "ideat-" which means "formed as an idea."[1]

Source: Conversation with Bing, 6/3/2023

(1) Ideate definition and meaning – Merriam-Webster. https://www.merriam-webster.com/dictionary/ideate.

(2) Ideate definition in the Cambridge English Dictionary. https://dictionary.cambridge.org/us/dictionary/english/ideate.

(3) https://bing.com/search?q=ideate+meaning.

(4) Ideate definition, meaning, and Usage – FineDictionary.com. https://www.finedictionary.com/ideate.

(5) Ideate English meaning – Cambridge Dictionary. https://dictionary.cambridge.org/dictionary/english/ideate.

Chapter 1

The Problem

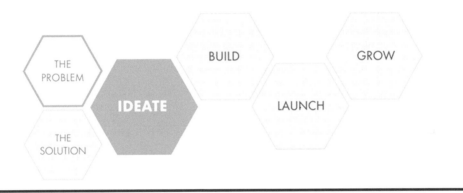

Figure 1.1 The problem.

Source: © Sally Ann Frank

This is a great idea for a digital health company!

You want to save the world. You are driven. You are bursting at the seams to make your mark and help people along the way. That's great. Really, it is. We need people like you to help evolve our healthcare system into a more reliable, equitable, effective, and efficient network. Here are some statistics to convey just how badly we need innovators; according to the World Health Organization,

> There is a 1 in a million chance of a person being harmed while traveling by plane. In comparison, there is a 1 in 300 chance of a patient being harmed during health care…It is estimated that from 5 to 50% of all medical errors in primary care are administrative errors.[1]

DOI: 10.4324/9781032639468-1

That same report continues, "Using conservative estimates, the latest data shows that patient harm is the 14th leading cause of morbidity and mortality across the world."[2]

Complicating matters are two significant factors. The first is the rising number of elderly people globally. The Center for Disease Control and Prevention (CDC) cites, "By 2040, the number of older adults is expected to reach 80.8 million. By 2060, it will reach 94.7 million, and older adults will make up nearly 25% of the US population."[3] The other major factor is the decreasing number of medical professionals. Again, in the United States, a Mercer 2021 healthcare labor report states that if current

> workforce trends hold, more than 6.5 million individuals will permanently leave these jobs within five years while only 1.9 million will step in to take their place. That adds up to a substantial shortage of critical healthcare labor in this country — coming up more than 3.2 million workers short within five years.[4]

While not great news for our healthcare system, it is excellent news for you. Your innovative mind and approach could be just the solution our healthcare delivery system needs. That's great, right? YES! But taking an idea and turning it into a profitable business starts by selecting a problem that can be solved, that people will pay you to solve for them. This may sound simple, but it isn't easy.

Here's an example from my own experience in technology sales. I once pitched an analytics dashboard to a prospect who had multiple people spending multiple days using spreadsheets to manually generate a beautiful dashboard that he presented to his leadership team at monthly meetings. The company where I worked was already working on a project with this organization but in another division. So, this fell into the "land and expand" approach (covered in Chapter 9, Go to Market (GTM) Strategy). Typically, an easier and faster sales process (I was already calculating my commission), I met with the prospect, carefully noting areas where I thought we could help him by increasing productivity and reducing costs. A couple of weeks later, we met again, and with my PowerPoint deck at the ready, I showed him how we could automate the dashboard by connecting directly to the data sources. I also highlighted that with our solution, the dashboard could be generated on-demand with the latest data at any time during the monthly reporting cycle. I told him (with great bravado) that he could repurpose his staff to higher-value tasks. Slam dunk, right? Uh, no. The customer looked me straight in the eye and said,

> I don't care about that. We've always done it this way, with these people for a long time and there is no business reason to change anything. My leadership team doesn't need the dashboard any sooner, and the monthly cadence has worked fine for years.

My whole value proposition meant nothing to him. I had never considered the possibility that he wasn't interested in what I had to offer. It was quite a painful lesson, indeed (and visions of my growing bank account disintegrated instantaneously).

Trying to solve the problems that plague our healthcare systems is far more complicated than my simple dashboard example. As a digital health founder, you have to consider many factors, unique to the industry:

- **Security** – keeping patient data, hospital technologies, and treatment systems secure and hacker-proof
- **Regulations** – following the laws that ensure technology is used safely according to government standards
- **Risk** – avoiding risks to lives and livelihoods, making sure that the new solution doesn't introduce additional risks
- **Equity** – ensuring patients get what they need as individuals, and access is not restricted
- **Bias** – understanding inherent biases in care, such as clinical trials or AI models used for clinical decision making and using technology to remove them as much as possible

With these industry-specific needs in mind, think about the problem you want to solve and if you can address these issues directly. Is this your idea or have you read about the problem in trade journals? Have you spoken to anyone who might be a prospective user and asked them about the problem? Do *they* think the problem needs to be solved and are they willing to *pay* you for it? This is where many people fall flat. Not doing the customer discovery to determine if customers are willing to go through the (often painful) change management process needed to adopt a solution.

At this point, you are officially in the ideation stage, typically characterized by the founder having an idea and beginning to formalize it in some way. This can be as simple as a drawing or schematic or as detailed as a business plan. The key here is that the founder's idea is unsubstantiated as a business. This is where customer discovery goes a long, long way. You're probably asking, "How can I do customer discovery without a product? And how do I find the right people to ask?" Proper customer interviews are both art and science, and you could hire professionals, but you may not be in a position to do so. So, what are your options? Here are a few:

■ **Interviews** – Find a small group of people (5–10) who represent your ideal customer. Ask them how they deal with the issue currently and get their feedback on your idea. These contacts shouldn't be relatives or friends. You don't need people to be nice; you need them to be critical. In fact, the more critical, the better. LinkedIn is a great tool for finding friends of friends who may be suitable. It's important to note that your interviews should be filled with diverse respondents from different geographic regions (limited to your initial rollout plans, US, Europe, etc.), different backgrounds, genders, longevity in the field, and different roles within your targeted customer organizations. For example, you don't want to ask only nurses, only to find that other clinicians, or administrators who often hold the purse strings, think differently. Once you have mapped out the buying journey (see below), you'll want to make sure the interviews include a few from each step within that journey.

■ **Polls** – Well-designed surveys or polls can be a great way to get immediate feedback. This is a common tactic, used by high school students to seasoned entrepreneurs. There are numerous (free!) tools out there and lots of guidance online about these feedback instruments.

■ **Research** – Yes, old-fashioned research about trends, industry gaps, and failed companies (and why) are all great sources to help you frame the problem you are trying to solve. While there are many sources available, and research companies you can subscribe to, I typically scan the internet for reputable industry sources and subscribe to organizations like Beckers (Becker's Hospital Review – Healthcare News (beckershospitalreview.com)), Health IT News (part of HIMSS), and trade organizations like HIMSS, HLTH, BIO-IT, and Drug Information Association. If you plan to use ChatGPT to streamline your research, be sure to check the citations provided and find some reputable ones of your own.

There are some guardrails for doing these types of inquiries, in addition to making sure you are not just asking people (friends and family) who will likely agree with you or say nice things, lest they hurt your feelings:

■ **Problem statement** – Clearly articulate the problem you are trying to solve. Resist the urge to use jargon, but instead, explain the problem as if your grandmother was your audience. Be as concise and straightforward as possible. Don't use acronyms, and especially don't use acronyms that you have, I'll say this gently, coined. I've had numerous founders develop acronyms for products and services to differentiate themselves, only to find it confuses their audience and turns prospects away. No one wants to feel stupid, so use common language everyone can grasp. This is true for the interviews and all the elements of the interviews, as you should consider these interactions rehearsals for how you will pitch your company.

■ **Artifact** – Use visuals that convey what your product will do. It can be a PowerPoint presentation that is a mockup of your user interface, a flowchart of your data flow, or a 3D printed version of your device, or all three, if they apply. The goal here is to augment your words with pictures, to capture and engage your audience, appealing to multiple senses and learning styles. Doing this now will prove valuable as you build your company.

■ **Value proposition** – This can be the most difficult to quantify, but in the ideation stage, you need not be focused on the total addressable market (TAM). You should look for your audience's response to the problem statement and artifact. Are they engaged? Excited? Bored? Begin asking open-ended questions to understand how important or worthwhile your solution could be for them. Pose questions like, "How are you dealing with this problem today?" "If you could resolve this issue, how would you do it?" "Tell me how you and your colleagues collaborate to deal with this problem." (More on the value proposition in Chapter 6, The Company.)

■ **Marketecture** – I know this is not technically a word (and yet spell-check accepted it!), but if your solution is dependent on technology, you'll want to include technical buyers (Chief Information Officers (CIOs), Chief Technical Officers (CTOs), etc.) in your interviews and have a general schematic (hence, marketecture) of your solution.

Be aware that in this regulated industry, your marketecture needs to convey the safeguards for security, privacy, and other industry-specific requirements.

- **Buying journey** – This is a BIG one often overlooked by newbies and seasoned entrepreneurs. Begin mapping out and confirming the buying process for your solution. Who will be involved? Who will be the decision makers and who will be the influencers? (More on these roles in Chapter 7, The Pitch.) Who has the budget to buy your solution? What level of customer support will be expected after the purchase? Are there follow-on products that can be sold? As you map out the buying journey, check in with your proxy customers and ensure that you are on the right track by posing these types of buying process questions to them. While every organization's buying process differs, there are similarities and similar steps to consider.

- **Competitors** – You must be willing to ask the question that you loathe to ask, namely, "Are you seeing other companies trying to solve this problem? If so, how are they doing? What's good or bad about their approach?" And remember, a customer considering doing nothing about the problem *is* competitive pressure, like my example above.

- **Focus** – This may seem self-evident, but staying focused on the problem you are trying to solve is harder than you think. Imagine this scenario: you finally get 30 minutes with someone you believe to be the archetype for your customer. She didn't respond to your numerous LinkedIn messages, but a friend introduced you, and here you are, virtually face-to-face, ready to share your idea. About ten minutes into the call, your dream proxy customer suggests solving another problem. Oh, your problem X is important too, but have you thought about trying to solve Y? Your gut tells you to be agreeable and say, sure, that's a great idea. I'll work that into my business plan. No, no, no. Unless you are prepared to drop your idea for hers, stick with what you started with. Acknowledge the value of her idea and tell her you are tucking her idea away for a potential growth opportunity down the line. If you are going to get through the ideation phase without going crazy, you need to be focused – hyper focused. Do your best to return the conversation to the problem you've already identified (politely, of course) and continue your mission.

Many organizations, including my own, have applied the Jobs to Be Done method from Clayton Christensen.

> When we buy a product, we essentially "hire" something to get
> a job done. If it does the job well, when we are confronted with
> the same job, we hire that same product again. And if the product
> does a crummy job, we "fire" it and look around for something else
> we might hire to solve the problem.[5]

It's a constructive way to look at solving a problem and takes into consideration much more than just how the product will function.

> [I]t also implies powerful social and emotional dimensions, underscoring the idea that the circumstances in which customers try to
> accomplish their intended goals are more critical than any buyer
> characteristics,[6]

according to an article John Marc Green wrote for Digital Health Insights. He goes onto say that in digital health,

> it's clear that defining the right problems and focusing on the "jobs"
> that need to be done will be key to driving innovation, especially
> in the realm of healthcare efficiency and quality improvement. By
> embracing this mindset, healthcare organizations can ensure they
> are tackling the right problems and delivering solutions that truly
> meet the needs of their patients, clinicians, and stakeholders.[7]

If you can hire a firm or person to conduct customer discovery, you can consider companies like Strategyzer (https://www.strategyzer.com/). They have proven methods and tools for effective customer discovery. Strategyzer has a book available, *Business Model Generation* (preview, download PDF, or buy on strategyzer.com) that enables you to take the journey on your own with their framework. I have used the book and modeling approach, facilitated by their team members, and I found it extremely helpful.

This is a lot to consider, but it's also essential to cultivate relationships with these proxy customers, as you will want the option to return to them in the future. Ideation is not a single moment in time. You will likely continue to iterate on how you will solve the problem multiple times, even through the process of developing your minimally viable product (MVP) and beyond. Customer discovery is never completed – it's just done for a particular milestone, and you will return to it repeatedly.

Summary

Pitfall	Best Practice
You develop your idea for a digital health solution in a vacuum	Vet your idea with proxy customers and ask: • Is this problem worth solving? • Will you pay to have it solved? • Who else is trying to solve this problem? • How would you solve it?

Resources

- Five Considerations For Finding Your Business Idea (forbes.com).
- How to Know Which Ideas Your Company Should Pursue (hbr.org).
- 10 Questions to Ask Yourself When Testing a Business Idea | Entrepreneur.
- Competing against Luck: The Story of Innovation and Customer Choice: Christensen, Clayton M., Dillon, Karen, Hall, Taddy, Duncan, David S.: 9780062435613: Amazon.com: Books.

Notes

1. Patient safety (who.int).
2. Patient safety (who.int).
3. Promoting Health for Older Adults | CDC.
4. us-2021-healthcare-labor-market-whitepaper.pdf (mercer.us).
5. Clayton Christensen: The Theory of Jobs To Be Done – HBS Working Knowledge.
6. Problem definition as a key to healthcare innovation – Digital Health Insights (dhinsights.org).
7. Problem definition as a key to healthcare innovation – Digital Health Insights (dhinsights.org).

Chapter 2

The Solution

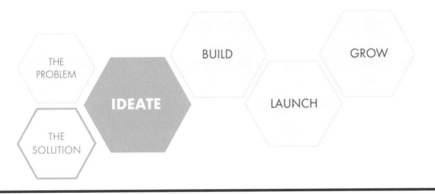

Figure 2.1   The solution.

Source: © Sally Ann Frank

I know exactly what I need to build.

A startup focusing on training clinicians to better care for a particular under-served population struggles to gain traction with customers. Their customers find the training content to be high-quality and seemingly effective. But there's a problem. The training portal is a partial solution, perhaps due to a lack of customer discovery. Customers are clamoring to understand the true value of the virtual training program. Without an analytic backend to the training portal, customers cannot measure the value of the training for their organization. They don't know how it affects their staff, patients, or bottom line. In several meetings with the startup founder and team, I stressed that not being able to quantify the benefits of the training program would likely lead to pilots of their solution that don't matriculate to a full production implementation (and accompanying revenue).

DOI: 10.4324/9781032639468-2   **9**

I suggested they add an analytic platform that conveys: how often the content is viewed, for how long, and by which roles; subsequent changes in patient journeys that save time or money; and reduced readmissions that improve outcomes and save money. These types of analytics provide customers with a qualitative return on investment, giving them the data they need to continually justify purchasing a particular solution.

Additionally, the startup is losing out on a potential revenue stream. Not only can the startup share the analytic data with its customer, but it can also monetize the data, charging "premium users" to compare their outcomes with others using the same training materials.

In Chapter 1, you confirmed that the problem you want to solve is worth solving. Proxy customers and your diligent research are pointing toward "all systems go." Terrific! It's time to get busy mapping out your solution.

As you've anticipated, designing your solution should also be in collaboration with key stakeholders. However, to properly design your solution, you will need to think in a structured, systematic way. Additionally, you will need to decide how to validate your approach, apply interoperability standards, and meet regulatory requirements. Things are getting more complicated, but that's standard fare for digital health startups. Unlike any other industry, healthcare and life sciences directly affect people's lives (and deaths). So, prepare to be comfortable with being uncomfortable.

The first consideration in building your new solution is to ask: is the underlying technology new or just repackaged old technology? Each of these scenarios will have very different paths. If your solution is based on existing technology, your path will be smoother and faster. Let's say you are building a solution that analyzes data from medical records in a new way. Customers, partners, and investors are familiar with that type of solution and generally know what to expect and how it can be used.

However, suppose your solution is cutting edge, using brand new technology, like generative AI (at this writing), or unique technology you are developing. In that case, your solution will be blazing a trail, requiring you to educate the market, build new adoption methods, and develop change management approaches for your customers (the full discussion about technology is in Chapter 4).

Let's start with the easier path: using existing, known technology in a new way. The main components of your solution (minus the actual technology) revolve around the data, the value generated, and the user experience.

Using Known Technology

Data is the primary driver of many successful digital health innovations. It is impossible to cover all aspects of what's happening with healthcare data, but the amount of healthcare data being generated is growing exponentially. According to a report by RBC Capital Market,[1] healthcare data is projected to grow faster than in manufacturing, financial services, or media. In 2017, it was estimated that with a single patient generating nearly 80 megabytes of data each year in imaging and EMR data, the compound annual growth rate (CAGR) of data for healthcare would reach 36% by 2025.[2] Additionally, the types and sources of data are also expanding to include wearables, imaging data, genomics, electronic medical records, prescription data, lifestyle data, exercise data… you get the idea. Furthermore, there are more and more ways to marry healthcare data with other types of data to get a complete picture of a patient, whether a retailer is pairing prescription data with other in-store purchases, or an insurer is incentivizing better eating habits by subsidizing grocery store purchases.

Value is the most esoteric part of your solution, as, like beauty, it can be subjective and in the eye of the beholder. To succeed in your business, value should be quantitative and qualitative, i.e., the analysis generated by your data-rich solution should reduce costs or improve revenue (as examples). Still, it should also be pleasing to the eye, easy to understand, and straightforward to adopt. Typical value statements turn your mission into a return on investment that is attractive and important to your target customers. Additionally, you should supply proof points, even if you don't have customers yet. Write the proof points you hope to have, enabling you to drive toward the desired outcome for you and your customers. Here's one example from a top Microsoft for Startups company, Hyro:

- **Mission** – Hyro equips healthcare organizations with a digital workforce of AI assistants, automating all routine calls and messages across their most valuable platforms, services, and channels – including call centers, websites, mobile apps, and SMS.[3]
- **Value statement** – Top-performing organizations trust Hyro's plug-and-play approach, including an award-winning natural language engine, to help them recapture time and investment lost to building and maintaining chat and voice solutions. With Conversational Intelligence, Hyro delivers omnichannel analytics, including engagement metrics, trending topics, and knowledge gaps, which offer industry-leading explainability,

control, and optimization. Headquartered in New York, Hyro delights clients like Intermountain Healthcare, Baptist Health, and Novant Health with AI assistants that are 60 times faster to deploy, easy to maintain and simple to scale – conserving vital resources while generating better conversations, more conversions, and revenue-driving insights.[4]

▪ Proof points

Figure 2.2   Proof points from Hyro.

Source: https://www.hyro.ai/.

As you can see, these proof points are stellar with key elements that drive the ROI narrative: a documented, executive-level customer; metrics that highlight savings and improvements in customer service; and qualitative descriptions about the experience these customers had working with Hyro.

Moving on to the customer experience, the user interface is the product for many of your prospective customers. Most of your customers, especially clinicians, staffers, scientists, or other non-IT people, don't know or care what happens behind their user interface. And at this point, you may be thinking about the technology, but you needn't have it all figured out yet. As you are still in the ideate stage, you want to clearly understand what

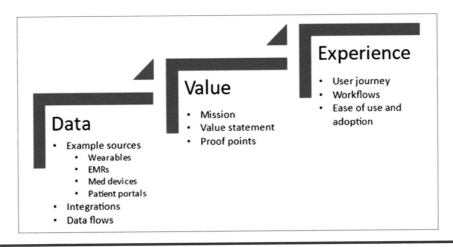

Figure 2.3   Elements of a customer journey.

Source: © Sally Ann Frank

the user journey should look like and how it integrates or changes current workflows.

At this point, mapping out wireframes of the user experience is one great way to document your thoughts and share them with proxy customers for their feedback. There are various tools designed just for this purpose, and you can get as basic as a flowchart in PowerPoint or as bespoke as in Figma (https://www.figma.com/). What's most important is selecting a tool you can easily update and share with your prospective customers. When mapping out your customer journey, include the following elements in the Figure 2.3.

Once you feel confident (mostly) about the data, value, and user experience, it's time to move on to other key considerations, such as interoperability, regulatory compliance, pilots, and solution validation. You may think tackling these topics at this point seems a bit premature, and it is – to an extent. However, the sooner you start considering these topics, the easier it will be later as your solution begins to take shape.

- **Interoperability** – "Point-solution fatigue" is real and rampant in healthcare and life sciences. Whether your customer is responsible for improving clinical trials or clinical visits, they don't want to add one more dashboard, report portal, or separate system to their workflows. Interoperability with electronic medical records (EMRs), clinical trial management systems (CTMS), and any existing systems they use will be key to your long-term success. Begin to inventory the types of systems your customers use today to understand how your system can integrate and work seamlessly with those systems. Your customers will thank you later (and buy your solution). More to come in Chapter 4, where technology is discussed in more detail.

- **Regulatory compliance** – Planning for regulatory compliance while still ideating is also a must-do. Regulatory compliance must be integral to mapping out your solution and not an afterthought. I have seen several startup founders skip over this, figuring they can work it in later. While there are several online sources detailing the regulations you need to consider, do your research based on what type of solution (medical device, software as a medical device, mobile app, etc.) and where you plan to launch your solution, as regulations vary from country to country. And be advised that the Health Insurance Portability and Accountability Act (HIPAA) in the United States and General Data Protection Regulation (GDPR) in the EU are just starting points. It's a good idea to begin identifying legal firms that have specialized knowledge in this area and who are accustomed to working with digital health startups. Compliance is not an area to tackle alone unless you, or someone you plan to hire, is a compliance expert. The fines are steep for failing to comply and can range from $100 to $1.5M[5] and up to 10 years in jail if found to be a criminal act.[6] One final point on compliance, I have seen some founders launch their solution as a "wellness" tool, which still requires HIPAA/GDPR compliance, but sidesteps many others. Nikhil Segal, the founder of Vastmindz (https://www.vastmindz.com/), brought their AI-based solution, which uses cell and webcams to generate biometrics like heart rate, blood pressure, and O2 saturation, to market as a wellness tool. Having launched in the wellness space with paying customers, they are now ready to begin their regulatory journey, including validation, for their solution as a clinical decision support tool.

- **Solution validation** – This is where you get your proxy customers and others involved to confirm that your solution will work as everyone expects. Again, at this point, this is more about planning than executing your validation process. Key considerations include: finding your clinical champions who will be early adopters; identifying academic medical centers (AMCs) whose mission and research areas align with your work; and conceptualizing how much of your solution will need to be built to enable clinicians or staff members to test it. Again, making these connections early, before you need them, will pay dividends when you are ready to test your MVP with proxy customers. There are a few established methods for testing solutions in AMCs and other provider organizations, such as IRBs:

Under FDA regulations, an Institutional Review Board is [a] group that has been formally designated to review and monitor biomedical research involving human subjects. In accordance with FDA regulations, an IRB has the authority to approve, require modifications in (to secure approval), or disapprove research. This group review serves an important role in the protection of the rights and welfare of human research subjects.[7]

■ **Pilots** – This brings us to pilots. Even if you are months away from your first pilot, as you begin to design your solution, identify how much of your solution needs to be completed before you can begin piloting it with prospective customers. Additionally, figure out what a pilot project, i.e., a small-scale implementation of your solution, looks like for you and your customer. Consider how long the pilot might run, how much it would cost, and what value the customer is likely to gain. While your ideal pilot project will likely change over time, having a baseline of the ideal scenario is critical to making it happen. Also, in formulating your pilot and strategy, remember to bake in added benefits for you in exchange for reduced prices for pilots for your customers. For example, you might offer a 20% discount to a pilot customer in exchange for a joint white paper or public case study (either written, video, or both). It's also important to structure your pilot to enable the solution to be tested and then validated by human experts, especially if your solution relies on artificial intelligence (AI). This approach is often termed human-augmented AI. In a recent video interview, John Halamka, MD, describes how risk plays a vital role in this approach and alludes to upcoming legislation that puts the clinician in the center of an AI solution.[8] Lastly, begin to identify how your successful pilot projects will transition into full-scale implementations. The last thing you want to do is to have a successful pilot only to be caught without a plan or the resources to move into production.

Using New(er) Technology

If you are a trailblazer and using nascent technology in your solution, all the items above apply, plus a few more challenges. Specifically, you will need to emphasize education and change management. To be successful, trailblazers need to evangelize their approach, the technology being used, and address any safety, security, and privacy concerns. How will you convey that your solution, with this innovative technology, is better than existing methods? How will you ensure that patient safety (and reduced liability) is at the forefront? How will you, as a founder of a small startup, begin to excite people about using this new tech?

When managing change, you will need to understand how adopting your solution may differ from other technology solutions that your customers have purchased in the past. Then, you will need to build a change management plan that makes implementing your solution as trouble-free and streamlined as possible. In an article from Forbes by Yoav Kutner, Five Steps to Successful Technology Change Management, he identifies five steps needed for change management:

1. Set and communicate clear goals
2. Build a team
3. Define a strategy
4. Plan for resistance
5. Ensure continuous improvement[9]

I particularly like that the author highlights the need to expect resistance and to be purposeful in developing the change management plan by setting communication goals and leaving room for continuous improvement.

The Business Model Gap

One of the most common gaps I see with founders is the lack of thought about what type of business model is well-suited for their solution. In the idea stage, it is probably too early to lock in how your customers will pay you, but it's important to begin the research now. Since this book (and you) are dedicated to digital health startups, you are likely building a software-as-a-service (SaaS) company. But that is just the starting point. How will you charge your customers? Will it be by user, transaction, analytic cycles, patient population, etc.? The other key element of the business model is your approach to supporting your customers. Again, as a SaaS digital health company, will you need 24/7 technical support? If so, will you hire or outsource it? How will those costs affect your profitability? While you don't need to have all the answers now, you do need to start researching companies like your company and understand their models. Also, look at companies that are successful (of course) and that you admire or aspire to emulate. We will share more information on business model development in Chapter 6, The Company.

Summary

Pitfall	Best Practice
You just start building your solution without considering key, non-technical aspects	Design your solution in non-technical terms • Consider regulations, security, and privacy • Detail the user experience • Map out needed integration • Plan for pilots and full production implementations • Remember to build change management and adoption processes

Resources

- Business Model Generation: A Handbook for Visionaries, Game Changers, and Challengers (The Strategyzer series): Osterwalder, Alexander, Pigneur, Yves: 9780470876411: Amazon.com: Books.
- Customer Understanding: Three Ways to Put the "Customer" in Customer Experience (and at the Heart of Your Business): Franz, Annette: 9781686886812
- The Disruption Mindset: Why Some Organizations Transform While Others Fail: Li, Charlene: 9781940858708: Books.
- Outside In: The Power of Putting Customers at the Center of Your Business: Manning, Harley, Bodine, Kerry, Bernoff, Josh: Kindle Store: eBook.

Notes

1. The healthcare data explosion – rbccm.com https://www.rbccm.com/en/gib/healthcare/episode/the_healthcare_data_explosion.
2. The Skyrocketing Volume of Healthcare Data Makes Privacy Imperative Forbes https://www.forbes.com/sites/forbestechcouncil/2021/08/06/the-skyrocketing-volume-of-healthcare-data-makes-privacy-imperative/.
3. Hyro Raises $20M in Series B Funding to Advance AI-Powered Communications for Healthcare | Healthcare IT Today.
4. Hyro Raises $20M in Series B Funding to Advance AI-Powered Communications for Healthcare | Healthcare IT Today.
5. https://www.ama-assn.org/practice-management/hipaa/hipaa-violations-enforcement.
6. https://www.hipaajournal.com/what-are-the-penalties-for-hipaa-violations-7096/.
7. https://www.fda.gov/about-fda/center-drug-evaluation-and-research-cder/institutional-review-boards-irbs-and-protection-human-subjects-clinical-trials.
8. AI in Clinical – The Human/ Machine Risk Balance https://youtu.be/53agtM-1W3BE?t=279.
9. https://www.forbes.com/sites/forbestechcouncil/2021/05/03/five-steps-to-successful-technology-change-management/?sh=167e02a26f0a.

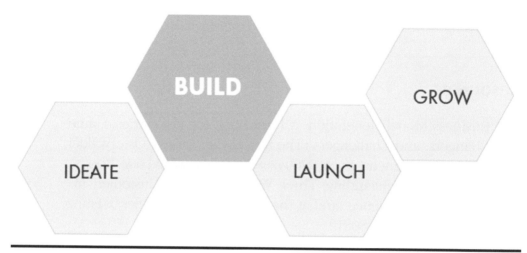

Figure 3.0   Build.

According to the Oxford Dictionary, "build" means "construct by putting parts or material together" as a verb.[1] It can also be used as a noun to refer to the dimensions or proportions of a person's or animal's body.[1]

Source: Conversation with Bing, 6/6/2023

(1) https://bing.com/search?q=build+definition.

Chapter 3

The Regulations

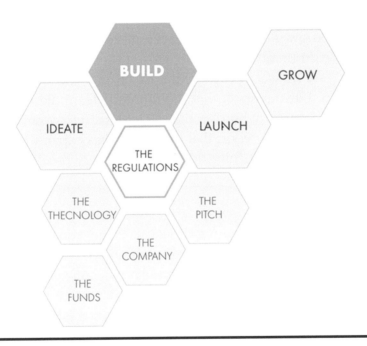

Figure 3.1   The regulations.

Source: © Sally Ann Frank

I'll figure out that regulatory stuff later.

During the Covid-19 pandemic, I advised a startup that was building a solution to enable diagnosis of Covid-19 by analyzing coughs. As the number of affected patients and deaths began to rise, the startup team thought their AI and machine learning model would quickly get emergency use authorization (EUA) from the Federal Drug Administration (FDA). They started their

DOI: 10.4324/9781032639468-3

regulatory journey in 2020 and applied for the EUA in September 2022. However, unable to complete the EUA process, in the spring of 2023, they embarked on another regulatory approach. The startup applied for de novo classification, meaning it would be evaluated as a new device with low to moderate risk and serve as a pre-cursor to a 510(k) submission (more on these designations later in this chapter). As I write this, the startup hopes to have its de novo status by the end of 2023.

This startup has interesting technology that could have helped flatten the curve during the pandemic. However, the regulatory journey stymied their ability to reach the marketplace in a timely manner. Now, the pandemic is (largely) behind us, and they still don't have their regulatory approval. While their product does still have relevance and they have built adjacent solutions, the sense of urgency has dissipated. Their solution is now a "nice to have," not a "must have."

While I don't know all the factors leading to the delay in regulatory approval, I did learn that the regulatory expert they hired wasn't as knowledgeable as he said he was. They spent a lot of time and money investing in the wrong expert. I also suspect that the founding team didn't have a complete view of the regulatory hurdles they would need to overcome.

However, I am happy to report that the startup has expanded its product set and is now on its way to launching additional (and very promising) solutions.

This doesn't have to be you. Now is the time to figure out your regulatory requirements and workflows. During the ideate stage, you were getting familiar with the types of regulations you need to consider. Now, as you begin your build, it's time to get serious about regulatory compliance – those that are must haves and those that may be optional but are important to customers.

Let's start with the single most important task in regulatory compliance – finding experts who can help. With the risks to health and safety at play here, unless you have a regulatory guru in your founding team or as an advisor, you will need help. Working with my Microsoft colleagues, we have put together a list of legal firms who can help startups through this journey (at startup friendly rates!). Most have global practices and can advise you regardless of your target market. Many offer initial consultations for free, which can be a great way to find the right regulatory partner. While I can't include my individual contacts at these firms, I can share the names of the firms themselves:

- Davis Wright Tremaine (https://www.dwt.com/)
- Dinsmore & Shohl (https://www.dinsmore.com/)

- Greenberg Traurig (https://www.gtlaw.com/en/)
- K&L Gates (https://www.klgates.com/)
- McDermott Will & Emery (https://www.mwe.com/)
- Perkins Coie (https://www.perkinscoie.com/en/)
- Reed Smith (https://www.reedsmith.com/en)

Again, this is not a guarantee of any sort about their services or what they offer. It is simply a list for you to consider and vet, instead of asking Bing or Google for a recommendation. Remember, if you find the right legal counsel, they will be a key member of your company, able to advise you on a variety of subjects, help you scale globally, and keep you out of trouble.

Just as you wouldn't turn your finances over to an accountant without keen oversight, it's important that you understand the regulations that will apply to you, your solution, and your company. The remainder of this chapter is focused on areas, as a founder or member of a founding team, you should consider during the build stage.

The first step is to understand, as best you can, what regulations will apply to your company and solution. There are regulations for data privacy, medical devices, software, information security, manufacturing, and quality, just to name a few. So, in this chapter we will cover the most common regulatory requirements.

Data Privacy

In healthcare, when dealing with data privacy, we are referring to HIPAA in the United States, GDPR in Europe, and PIPEDA in Canada.

- **HIPAA (United States)** – The Healthcare Information Portability and Accountability Act (HIPAA), is designed to help protect PHI, or patient health information. According to the CDC,

  A major goal of the Privacy Rule is to make sure that individuals' health information is properly protected while allowing the flow of health information needed to provide and promote high-quality healthcare, and to protect the public's health and well-being. The Privacy Rule permits important uses of information while protecting the privacy of people who seek care and healing.[1]

HIPAA compliance also requires organizations to establish Business Associate Agreements (BAA) with service providers that are accessing PHI. For example, if you plan to deploy your solution and will have access to PHI, you will need to sign a BAA with your hospital system customer. Since BAAs are standard practice, you will need to make sure that you fully understand their implications and can generate and adhere to BAAs for all your customers. A sample BAA can be found here, <u>Model Business Associate Agreement (hhs.gov)</u>.

Additionally, companies that plan to work with data from patients or consumers in California, need to comply with the California Consumer Privacy Act (CCPA), which gives consumers more control over the personal information that businesses collect about them and the CCPA regulations provide guidance on how to implement the law. This landmark law secures new privacy rights for California consumers, including:

- The right to know about the personal information a business collects about them and how it is used and shared;
- The right to delete personal information collected from them (with some exceptions);
- The right to opt-out of the sale or sharing of their personal information; and
- The right to non-discrimination for exercising their CCPA rights.[2]

In January 2023, additional provisions were introduced:

- The right to correct inaccurate personal information that a business has about them; and
- The right to limit the use and disclosure of sensitive personal information collected about them.[3]

- **GDPR (Europe)** – General Data Protection Regulation is also designed to protect patients and their data, though the subordinate details are different and more stringent. It includes data protection, accountability, data security, consent, and other elements.[4] It's important to note that in the UK,

the GDPR is retained in domestic law as the UK GDPR, but the UK has the independence to keep the framework under review. The "UK GDPR" sits alongside an amended version of the DPA [Data Protection Act] 2018.[5]

Perhaps the starkest contrast between HIPAA and GDPR is the elements of rights afforded to the individuals, or patients in this scenario, namely:

- The right to be informed
- The right of access
- The right to rectification
- The right to erasure
- The right to restrict processing
- The right to data portability
- The right to object
- Rights in relation to automated decision making and profiling

■ **PIPEDA (Canada)** – The Personal Information Protection and Electronic Documents Act (PIPEDA) covers similar data privacy areas.

Organizations covered by PIPEDA must generally obtain an individual's consent when they collect, use, or disclose that individual's personal information. People have the right to access their personal information held by an organization. They also have the right to challenge its accuracy. Personal information can only be used for the purposes for which it was collected. If an organization is going to use it for another purpose, they must obtain consent again. Personal information must be protected by appropriate safeguards.[6]

But HIPAA, GDPR, and PIPEDA only cover part of the world. The United Nations Conference on Trade and Development (UNCTAD) has an interactive map, shown in Figure 3.2, that shows which countries have data privacy legislation, plus a handy spreadsheet that you can download, that lists relevant legislation by country.[7] It's a helpful tool to quickly know the data privacy laws with which you will need to comply.

Medical Devices

If you think data privacy regulations are tricky, we are just getting started. When it comes to medical devices, there are a variety of regulatory pathways, depending on the type of solution you are building. I will focus largely on the US regulations for medical devices, as many of the startups I work with are most interested in the US market, regardless of where the company is based. We will also cover high-level information for Europe, the UK, Singapore, and Israel, as a sampling to show how similar and different

Figure 3.2   UN Map of regulations.

Source: https://unctad.org/page/data-protection-and-privacy-legislation-worldwide

regulations can be. I cannot stress enough that this information is just a starting point. You must engage with regulatory experts, as you begin building your solution, to ensure that you fully understand and follow the regulations that will be the guardrails for your solution and company.

United States

In the United States, the regulatory authority for medical devices is the Federal Drug Administration (FDA) and it has identified 16 specialty areas by which medical device classes are determined, as shown in Figure 3.3.[8]

Once you have identified your specialty area and have reviewed the regulation citation with your legal team or FDA expert, you'll work together to determine the type of medical device you are building, based on the classes of medical devices. The FDA regulation states:[9]

> *Class I* means the class of devices that are subject
> only to the general controls authorized by or under
> sections 501 (adulteration), 502 (misbranding), 510
> (registration), 516 (banned devices), 518 (notification
> and other remedies), 519 (records and reports), and

Medical Specialty		Regulation Citation (21CFR)
73	Anesthesiology	Part 868
74	Cardiovascular	Part 870
75	Chemistry	Part 862
76	Dental	Part 872
77	Ear, Nose, and Throat	Part 874
78	Gastroenterology and Urology	Part 876
79	General and Plastic Surgery	Part 878
80	General Hospital	Part 880
81	Hematology	Part 864
82	Immunology	Part 866
83	Microbiology	Part 866
84	Neurology	Part 882
85	Obstetrical and Gynecological	Part 884
86	Ophthalmic	Part 886
87	Orthopedic	Part 888
88	Pathology	Part 864
89	Physical Medicine	Part 890
90	Radiology	Part 892
91	Toxicology	Part 862

Figure 3.3   **FDA specialty areas for medical devices.**

Source: https://www.fda.gov/medical-devices/classify-your-medical-device/device-classification-panels

520 (general provisions) of the Federal Food, Drug, and Cosmetic Act. A device is in class I if:

(1) General controls are sufficient to provide reasonable assurance of the safety and effectiveness of the device, or

(2) There is insufficient information from which to determine that general controls are sufficient to provide reasonable assurance of the safety and effectiveness of the device or to establish special controls to provide such assurance, but the device is not life-supporting or life-sustaining, or for a use which is of substantial importance in

preventing impairment of human health, and which does not present a potential unreasonable risk of illness or injury.

Class II means the class of devices that is or eventually will be subject to special controls. A device is in class II if general controls alone are insufficient to provide reasonable assurance of its safety and effectiveness and there is sufficient information to establish special controls, including the promulgation of performance standards, postmarket surveillance, patient registries, development and dissemination of guidelines (including guidelines for the submission of clinical data in premarket notification submissions in accordance with section 510(k) of the Federal Food, Drug, and Cosmetic Act), recommendations, and other appropriate actions as the Commissioner deems necessary to provide such assurance. For a device that is purported or represented to be for use in supporting or sustaining human life, the Commissioner shall examine and identify the special controls, if any, which are necessary to provide adequate assurance of safety and effectiveness, and describe how such controls provide such assurance.

Class III means the class of devices for which premarket approval is or will be required in accordance with section 515 of the Federal Food, Drug, and Cosmetic Act. A device is in class III if insufficient information exists to determine that general controls are sufficient to provide reasonable assurance of its safety and effectiveness, or that application of special controls described in the definition of "*Class II*" in this section in addition to general controls, would provide such assurance, and if, in addition, the device is life-supporting or life-sustaining, or for a use which is of substantial importance in preventing impairment of human health, or if the device presents a potential unreasonable risk of illness or injury.

But to make this a bit easier to digest, here's a summary in plain English:

- **Class I** devices have the lowest risk and are typically everyday items, like stethoscopes. The FDA specifically states,

  Class I devices are not intended for use in supporting or sustaining life or to be of substantial importance in preventing impairment to human health, and they may not present a potential unreasonable risk of illness or injury.[10]
- **Class II** devices carry a bit more risk and may also be common items. I have Class II devices in my eyes – contact lenses.
- **Class III** devices carry the greatest risk, and we often think of implanted devices, like pacemakers, as Class III devices, although this is just one type.

There is yet another distinction to consider, FDA *approved* versus FDA *cleared*. CNET contributor, Sarah Mitroff, sums up the difference between the two:

  "FDA approved" means that the agency has determined that the "benefits of the product outweigh the known risks for the intended use." Manufacturers must submit a premarket approval (PMA) application *and* the results of clinical testing in order to get approval.

  Class II and Class I medical devices are usually "cleared" by the FDA, which means the manufacturer can demonstrate that their product is "substantially equivalent to another (similar) legally marketed device" that already has FDA clearance or approval. Those already-cleared products are called a predicate.[11]

Sonavi Labs, a startup that is bringing a category-leading digital stethoscope to market called Feelix, earned FDA *approval as a Class II medical device*. A traditional stethoscope was used as the predicate device against which Feelix was evaluated. The approval letter says in part:

  the device is substantially equivalent (for the indications for use stated in the enclosure) to legally marketed predicate devices marketed in interstate commerce prior to May 28, 1976, the enactment date of the Medical Device Amendments, or to devices that have been reclassified in accordance with the provisions of the Federal Food, Drug, and Cosmetic Act (Act) that do not require approval of a premarket approval application (PMA).[12]

If you are interested in reading the entire letter, you can do so here: https://www.accessdata.fda.gov/cdrh_docs/pdf20/K200862.pdf. Not only is it helpful to have a concrete example of the ruling from the FDA, but the background materials that Sonavi Labs submitted are also included in the document, enabling you to see what is needed to apply to the FDA.

There is one more facet to the FDA journey that you may travel, providing you with yet another way to classify your medical device:

- **Premarket approval (PMA)** – Most Class III (high risk) devices require premarket approval (PMA) before they may be legally marketed.
- **Premarket notification 510(k)** – Most Class II (moderate risk) devices require 510(k) clearance from the FDA before they may be legally marketed.
- **De novo** – De novo provides a possible route to classify novel devices of low to moderate risk.
- **Humanitarian device exemption (HDE)** – HDE provides a possible route to market medical devices that may help people with rare diseases or conditions.[13]

Europe and the UK

In Europe, a CE (an acronym for the French "Conformité Européenne") mark certifies that a product has met EU health, safety, and environmental requirements, which ensure consumer safety. Manufacturers in the European Union (EU) and abroad must meet CE marking requirements where applicable to market their products in Europe.[14]

In the European Union (EU) medical devices ensure they are safe and perform as intended through a regulated conformity assessment. These assessments are regulated at the country level, but the single European Medicines Agency (EMA) is involved in the regulatory process. The conformity assessment typically involves an audit of the manufacturer's quality system plus technical documentation reviews and evaluation of the safety and performance of the device. EMA breaks down the types of medical devices this way:

- **Medicines used in combination with a medical device** — EMA assesses the safety and effectiveness of medicines used in combination with a medical device.
- **Medical devices with an ancillary medicinal substance** — the notified body must seek EMA's scientific opinion on the quality, safety, and usefulness of the ancillary medicinal substance in three cases: if the ancillary substance is derived from human blood or plasma; if it has been previously evaluated by the EMA; or if it falls within the mandatory scope of the centralized procedure.
- **Companion diagnostics ("in vitro diagnostics")** — the notified body must seek EMA's scientific opinion on the suitability of the companion diagnostic to the medicinal product if the latter falls within the scope of the centralized procedure.
- **Medical devices made of substances that are systemically absorbed** — the notified body must seek the scientific opinion of a competent authority. The EMA provides scientific opinions on the compliance of the substance with the requirements laid down in Annex I to Directive 2001/83/EC.
- **High-risk medical devices** — EMA supports the medical device expert panels that provide opinions and views to notified bodies on the scientific assessment of certain high-risk medical devices and in vitro diagnostics.[15]

UK

Since 1 January 2021, there have been several changes in how medical devices are placed on the market in Great Britain (England, Wales, and Scotland). Summarized from their government website, they include:

- A new route to market and product marking (the UKCA marking) is available for manufacturers wishing to place medical devices on the Great Britain market
- All medical devices, including in vitro diagnostic medical devices (IVDs), custom-made devices and systems or procedure packs, need to be registered with the MHRA before they are placed on the Great Britain market
- If you are a medical device manufacturer based outside the UK and wish to place a device on the Great Britain market, you need to appoint a single UK Responsible Person for all

of your devices, who will act on your behalf to carry out specified tasks, such as registration. Further detail on the UK Responsible Person is set out below

■ Currently, CE marked medical devices with a valid CE marking can be placed on the Great Britain market until 30 June 2023. A valid CE marking is a CE marking that enables the medical device to be placed on the EU market. However, subject to Parliamentary approval, we intend to introduce measures before 30 June 2023 which will provide that CE marked medical devices may be placed on the Great Britain market to the following timelines:

– General medical devices compliant with the EU medical devices directive (EU MDD) or EU active implantable medical devices directive (AIMDD) with a valid declaration and CE marking can be placed on the Great Britain market up until the sooner of expiry of certificate or 30 June 2028

– In vitro diagnostic medical devices (IVDs) compliant with the EU in vitro diagnostic medical devices directive (IVDD) can be placed on the Great Britain market up until the sooner of expiry of certificate or 30 June 2030, and

– General medical devices including custom-made devices, compliant with the EU medical devices regulation (EU MDR) and IVDs compliant with the EU in vitro diagnostic medical devices regulation (EU IVDR) can be placed on the Great Britain market up until 30 June 2030.[16]

In February 2021, the UK's National Health Service (NHS) digital technology agency, NHSX,

launched the Digital Technology Assessment Criteria (DTAC), which consolidates existing legislation and principles of good practice into an easy to navigate set of baseline standards. DTAC will guide digital technology or app developers as they design or configure products for use in the NHS in England and help local or national health and social care organizations procure in line with NHS standards. The assessment criteria are divided into five components: clinical safety, data protection, technical assurance, interoperability, and usability and accessibility.[17]

Singapore

I chose to include Singapore in this overview as I've seen several startups, after doing market research, select Singapore as their first target in the Asia Pacific (APAC) market. Global accounting firm, Crowe, outlines the tax structure, innovation climate, and intellectual property (IP) protection as just a few of the reasons many companies from around the world, enter the Singapore market.[18]

In Singapore,

> medical devices are regulated under the Health Products Act and Health Products (Medical Devices) regulations. Singapore's Health Sciences Authority (HSA) oversees the system of statutory control aimed to safeguard the quality, safety, and efficacy of medical devices available in Singapore. Almost all medical devices are regulated. Class A medical devices supplied in a non-sterile state are exempted, however, Class A sterile, Class B, C, and D medical devices are subject to product registration requirements. Classification rules are adopted from the guidance developed by the Global Harmonization Task Force (GHTF).
>
> ASEAN has been developing a uniform system for registering and assessing medical devices across the ten-member countries. Various ASEAN economies have started adopting the ASEAN Medical Device Directive (AMDD). This requires ASEAN countries to adopt uniform classification criteria for medical devices. This bodes well for U.S. medical device manufacturers as they will be able to easily access a common medical device market with a market size of more than 600 million people. Adherence to the basic principles of the AMDD in ASEAN will likely take place over the next few years.[19]

Israel

Israel is another country that is teeming with innovation and partnerships with US healthcare, life sciences, and medical device companies. Israel is often referred to as, "startup nation," from the title of a book, *StartUp Nation: The Story of Israel's Economic Miracle* by Dan Senor and Saul Singer about the innovative, fast-paced Israeli economy.[20] But there's another benefit to working in the Israeli market, namely the accelerated pathway to compliance for companies able to submit existing FDA documentation.

Israeli medical device regulations state,

> for any imported medical device, the Israeli importer/agent must submit a registration application to MoH, Department of Medical Devices. The application should include (if available) a certificate issued by a competent authority of one of the following countries: Australia, Canada, European Community (CE) Member States (MSs), Japan, or the U.S. If such a certificate is not available, the registration process may still be available in some cases (usually for lower regulatory class devices) but will take longer, between two and six months, and the Minister of Health (MoH) will determine what type of testing is needed.
>
> Product registration supported by existing FDA documentation usually takes approximately four months. The application for registration of a medical device shall be submitted to the Department of Medical Devices at the MoH.[21]

Change Management for Medical Devices

A few years ago, I was at a meeting with executives from Microsoft (where I work) and Johnson & Johnson (J&J). At the time, I was part of the Internet of Things (IoT) team, focused on our top healthcare customers in the Americas. As our vice president of IoT engineering was briefing a particular division of J&J, the c-level executive from J&J asked, how do we manage software updates to our existing medical devices now that they all (or soon will) have a software component? Being the "expert" in the room, the Microsoft VP turned to me, propelling the question (and all eyes) to me. At the time, there was no good answer. While we had the technology to manage these types of updates, the FDA had not caught up, and there was no regulatory framework to perform these updates in a compliant manner. I'm happy to say in early 2023, the FDA issued its, "Draft Guidance on Predetermined Change Control Plans (PCCP) for Artificial Intelligence/ Machine Learning-Enabled Medical Devices,"[22] providing a framework for software updates to medical devices.

I strongly urge you to read more about it, but the gist of the PCCP is to increase patients' access to safe and effective medical devices. The plan would include a detailed description of the specific, planned device modifications; a description of the methodology that would be used to develop, validate, and implement those modifications; and a summary of the expected impact of the modifications on the device.[23]

Software

Software as a Medical Device (SaMD) is permeating all aspects of healthcare and life sciences, from clinical decision support systems to automated laboratory management systems. SaMD is defined by the International Medical Device Regulators Forum (IMDRF) as "software intended to be used for one or more medical purposes that perform these purposes without being part of a hardware medical device."[24]

The FDA provides guidance for clinical evaluation of Software as a Medical Device (SaMD) and is intended to help industry and FDA staff understand the FDA's recommendations for clinical evaluation of SaMD.[25] The guidance focuses on principles of clinical evaluation, which include establishing the scientific validity, clinical performance, and analytical validity for SaMD. The guidance also describes an internally agreed upon understanding of clinical evaluation and principles for demonstrating the safety, effectiveness, and performance of Software as a Medical Device among regulators in the International Medical Device Regulators Forum.[26]

Examples of SaMD include the software bundled with medical devices, imagining systems, and clinical decision support tools. The FDA defines SaMD as:

- Software used to "drive or control" the motors and the pumping of medication in an infusion pump; or software used in closed loop control in an implantable pacemaker or other types of hardware medical devices. These types of software, sometimes referred to as "embedded software", "firmware", or "micro-code" are not Software as a Medical Device.
- Software required by a hardware medical device to perform the hardware's medical device intended use, even if sold separately from the hardware medical device.

- Software that relies on data from a medical device, but does not have a medical purpose, e.g., software that encrypts data for transmission from a medical device.
- Software that enables clinical communication and workflow including patient registration, scheduling visits, voice calling, and video calling.
- Software that monitors performance or proper functioning of a device for the purpose of servicing the device, (e.g., software that monitors x-ray tube performance to anticipate the need for replacement), or software that integrates and analyzes laboratory quality control data to identify increased random errors or trends in calibration on IVDs.
- Software that provides parameters that become the input for software as a medical device is not software as a medical device if it does not have a medical purpose. For example, a database including search and query functions by itself or when used by Software as a Medical Device.[27]

If you are interested in the SaMD regulations in Europe, IQVIA has recently produced a 2-part white paper series, <u>Regulations and Reimbursement of Software as a Medical Device in Europe – Part 1 – IQVIA</u> and <u>Regulations and Reimbursement of Software as a Medical Device in Europe Part 2 – IQVIA</u>. Again, don't assume that by reading a few white papers you will be ready to tackle SaMD. But do find reliable sources like these and share them with your trusted regulatory advisor.

Manufacturing and Good Practice (GxP)

While most of the digital health solutions are heavily weighted toward software, there are often medical devices, labs, and manufacturing processes which must adhere to global GxP regulations. Additionally, pharmaceutical and life sciences companies must also follow these standards.

> The term *GxP* is a general abbreviation for "good practice" guidelines and regulations. The "x" represents a particular field—clinical (GCP), manufacturing (GMP), distribution (GDP), laboratory (GLP), agriculture (GAP), and so on. There is no single regulatory entity or administration; each country has its own guidelines and

regulators, although requirements are similar from country to country. GxP regulations include those requirements outlined in the US Food and Drug Administration (FDA) CFR Title 21 Part 11 and EudraLex Volume 4—GMP Guidelines, Annex 11 in the European Union (EU).

Regulatory goals aim to make sure that businesses in regulated industries manufacture products that are safe to use and meet stringent quality standards during the production process. Computerized systems that use GxP processes require validation of adherence to GxP requirements and are considered qualified when the system can demonstrate its ability to fulfill them.[28]

Summary

Pitfall	Best Practice
You postpone learning about regulations that will affect building and selling your solution	Begin preparing for your regulatory journey now • Develop a working knowledge of key regulations that apply to your solution in your target markets • Identify and begin engaging with regulatory experts who will support your regulatory process

Resources (In Addition to the Many Endnotes)

■ HITRUST Alliance | Information Risk Management and Compliance.
■ Automated SOC 2, HIPAA, GDPR, Risk Management, & More | Drata.
■ ECM Software & GxP Services for Life Science | Montrium.
■ The Current State of 521 FDA-Approved, AI-Based Medical Devices | LinkedIn.

Notes

1. Health Insurance Portability and Accountability Act of 1996 (HIPAA) | CDC.
2. California Consumer Privacy Act (CCPA) | State of California – Department of Justice – Office of the Attorney General.
3. California Consumer Privacy Act (CCPA) | State of California – Department of Justice – Office of the Attorney General.

4. What Is GDPR, the EU's New Data Protection Law? - GDPR.eu.
5. The UK GDPR | ICO.
6. PIPEDA in Brief – Office of the Privacy Commissioner of Canada.
7. Data Protection and Privacy Legislation Worldwide | UNCTAD.
8. Device Classification Panels | FDA.
9. CFR – Code of Federal Regulations Title 21 (fda.gov).
10. General Controls for Medical Devices | FDA.
11. FDA Approved vs. FDA Cleared: Why You Need to Know the Difference (cnet .com).
12. https://www.accessdata.fda.gov/cdrh_docs/pdf20/K200862.pdf.
13. How to Determine If Your Product Is a Medical Device | FDA.
14. CE Marking (trade.gov).
15. Medical Devices | European Medicines Agency (europa.eu).
16. Regulating Medical Devices in the UK – GOV.UK (www.gov.uk).
17. UK NHS Digital Technology Assessment Criteria (trade.gov).
18. 10 Reasons Why Singapore Is an Attractive Investment Destination.
19. Singapore - Healthcare (trade.gov).
20. How Israel Became A Technology Startup Nation (forbes.com).
21. Healthcare Resource Guide – Israel (trade.gov).
22. CDRH Issues Draft Guidance on Predetermined Change Control Plans for Artificial Intelligence/Machine Learning-Enabled Medical Devices | FDA.
23. https://www.fda.gov/regulatory-information/search-fda-guidance-documents/ marketing-submission-recommendations-predetermined-change-control-plan -artificial.
24. Software as a Medical Device (SaMD) | FDA.
25. AIML_SaMD_Action_Plan (fda.gov).
26. https://www.fda.gov/files/medical%20devices/published/Software-as-a-Medical -Device-%28SAMD%29--Clinical-Evaluation---Guidance-for-Industry-and-Food -and-Drug-Administration-Staff.pdf.
27. What Are Examples of Software as a Medical Device? | FDA.
28. Good Clinical, Laboratory, and Manufacturing Practices (GxP) – Microsoft Compliance | Microsoft Learn.

Chapter 4

The Technology

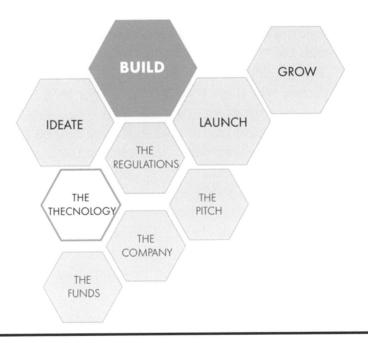

Figure 4.1   The technology.

Source: © Sally Ann Frank

I'll use this technology because that's what I know.

I was meeting with a startup that had a digital front door solution and learned that their architecture was spread across two different cloud vendors. Their reasoning was that they were able to bring the best of each vendor into their solution. They also liked not having their proverbial "eggs in one basket." Frankly, this isn't a bad strategy, and many enterprises are

DOI: 10.4324/9781032639468-4

multi-cloud. However, as a startup with much more limited resources, it's a different story. Staffing, DevOps, training, and onboarding customers all get much more complicated.

Furthermore, when it was time to go big with larger provider customers, the startup found the architecture lacked the security rigor their large provider customers wanted, relegating the company to working with smaller, regional providers (which is fine, if that is your sales strategy, but that was not the case here). Additionally, the startup wanted to investigate applying generative AI, and the leading tool was on a third platform. Imagine trying to grow a business; managing, staffing, and training for three different cloud environments; and convincing customers that the architecture isn't risky – all at once.

For many digital health founders, working with the technology is their favorite part of the journey. It's so empowering and rewarding to see a vision come to life through the wonders of bits and bytes. But selecting the technology platform is not a decision you should make lightly. What cloud and technology you choose will affect your business, your level of success, your customers, and your employees for years to come.

Before digging in, it's important to note that there will be new products and services entering the market, which may change the landscape of the industry. A year ago, few of us had heard of generative AI or OpenAI, and yet here we are – all talking about it trying to figure out how it fits into our work. With that in mind, I will provide overviews, but not extreme detail on specific technologies, as that will change. Instead, I will shed some light on the companies behind them and what you, as a digital health founder, might find attractive about working with each of the companies.

The Options

In much of the world, there are three primary cloud vendors, Amazon Web Services (AWS), Google Cloud Platform (GCP), and Microsoft Azure. Let me stipulate that I work at Microsoft, but I will try to leave my allegiance behind and share details about all three cloud vendors with as much equanimity as possible. Additionally, there are smaller organizations that cater to the startup industry by offering cloud services bundled with solution development services, like 3B Cloud, but I'll get to that later.

Most of the startup founders tell me that their technology selection is not well-researched. In fact, most non-technical founders give their tech stack little thought. Based on my own experience and research from my team, the decision is usually based on the need for speed, selecting the tool suite that the first technical hire knows well. Unfortunately, that first hire may be a CIO/CTO, or they may be a junior developer. And if that person leaves the company, you could be in a heap of trouble.

AWS

AWS excels in supplying digital health startups with their infrastructure. In fact, many of the startups I meet are on AWS. They do a terrific job in evangelizing their technology and have a strong brand image. Their commitment to healthcare is underscored by their latest acquisition of One Medical, adding both virtual and in-person care to Amazon's arsenal of healthcare solutions.[1] It is these types of acquisitions that make AWS both a solid choice for digital health founders and one that may have additional risk. They clearly understand healthcare, but will your business be the next to be cannibalized? And is that a consideration that a startup founder needs to consider? That's your call.

AWS, like the other cloud vendors, has all the building blocks that you need to be successful. They have customers in provider, payer, pharma, and med tech sectors and a robust ecosystem of partners. However, if you are targeting retail health, AWS may not be your best option, due to keen competition between AWS and health retailers, especially in the United States.

One of the differentiators to note about AWS is that in addition to their startup program (https://aws.amazon.com/startups/) they frequently run accelerator programs, some of which are geared specifically for healthcare and life sciences founders. In November of 2022, they launched a Healthcare Accelerator Global Cohort for Workforce Development program with the goal of, "driving new digital solutions for the global healthcare workforce," specifically by supporting innovation to "focus on training, retaining, and deploying healthcare workers."[2]

According to Investopedia, retail remains Amazon's primary source of revenue, with online and physical stores together accounting for the biggest share. Amazon Web Services (AWS) currently generates the majority of Amazon's operating *profits* (emphasis added) and is growing at a robust pace.[3] In 2021, AWS generated $62.2 billion in revenue[4] and in 2022, AWS generated $21.4 billion in sales.[5] However, according to Forbes writers, Steve Dennis[6] and Jason Goldberg,[7] as of February 2022, advertising was Amazon's top profit-making business for the company.

GCP

Only occasionally do I hear from startup founders that GCP is the cloud of choice and that they are members of the Google startup program (https://cloud.google.com/startup). It does happen, but if I were to rank the major cloud vendors by popularity in the startup ecosystem based on my experience, GCP would be last. Additionally, it is even more uncommon (again, based on my very *unscientific* survey) that the entire startup's solution is built on GCP. More often, one or more components of the Google cloud are integrated into a larger architecture that contains elements from AWS, Azure, or both.

While GCP also has similar technologies to offer, there are a few areas where they (at this writing) lag a bit behind AWS and Azure. For example, I was able to find remote patient architectures (see below) for both AWS and Azure, but not GCP. On the other hand, there may be elements of GCP that do make it a potential fit for some startups. For example, their ownership of Fitbit could represent an opportunity for startups that rely on wearables in their solutions.

According to Statista, Google Search is by far the biggest revenue segment of Alphabet.[8] In 2022, Alphabet's revenue from Google websites (including YouTube advertising) amounted to around $191B.[9] In 2020, the company generated $104B in "search and other" revenues, making up 71% of Google's ad revenue and 57% of Alphabet's total revenue.[10]

Microsoft Azure

Clearly, I know this technology stack the best. But in the spirit of fairness, I will concede that when recruiting startups for our program, I rarely talk about our technology – except when it comes to OpenAI and Azure OpenAI. Currently, we have a slight advantage in using and deploying large language models in health and life sciences, but this is a brand new area for the industry and still unchartered. How the AI arms race will evolve is still uncertain.

What I can tell you is that many founders I meet build on Microsoft technology, join our startup program (https://www.microsoft.com/en-us/startups), or move to Azure based on choices related to security, productivity tools (like PowerBI, Teams, GitHub, Co-pilots, etc.), and the Nuance acquisition. Founders are also eager to be part of the Microsoft Cloud for Healthcare offering, which leading partner Avanade summarizes as, "a fully integrated suite of solutions, including Azure, Microsoft 365, Dynamics 365, Microsoft Teams and Power Platform, designed to support your healthcare industry challenges."[11]

According to Investopedia, Microsoft's intelligent cloud segment is the largest source of profit, as well as the fastest-growing. Microsoft sells computing devices, cloud systems and services, software, and other products to consumers and businesses.[12] When we do a breakdown by product streams, the largest source of Microsoft's revenue was Office, with $44.9 billion (23% of the total). Just behind in the second place was Azure with $44bn of revenue (22% of total).[13] In 2022, Microsoft Cloud (formerly commercial cloud) revenue increased 32% to $91.2 billion.[14]

Going Deeper

Now that we've delved into the various business models there are some programmatic similarities that go across all three cloud providers, including a formal startup program, venture capital funding, and a partner program for startups once they complete the startup program.

Cloud	Startup Program	Investment Arm	Partner Program
AWS	https://aws.amazon.com/startups/	Various investment funds	AWS Partner Network
GCP	https://cloud.google.com/startup	Google Ventures	Google Partners
Microsoft Azure	https://www.microsoft.com/en-us/startups	M12	Microsoft Cloud Partner Program

These programs are important to founders like you, but are not the only considerations. Going a bit deeper into healthcare-specific factors, the Frost & Sullivan overview of healthcare use cases in Figure 4.2 is helpful in determining which cloud provider is likely to be most aligned with the solution you are building. However, you may want to consider these use cases from two sides: where you could align with existing approaches, or conversely, where you may be able to fill a gap that a cloud provider has.

Lastly, instead of trying to conduct a full technical comparison, let me point you to comparisons that have been completed by the experts:

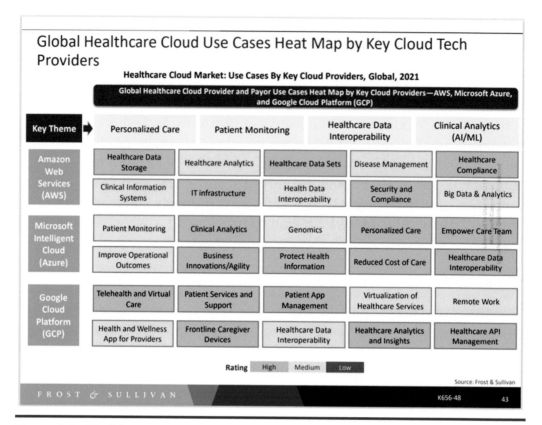

Figure 4.2 Healthcare uses cases.

Source: Global Healthcare Cloud Growth Opportunities (frost.com)

■ AWS and Azure services to Google Cloud https://cloud.google.com/docs
/get-started/aws-azure-gcp-service-comparison
■ Google Cloud to Azure services comparison https://learn.microsoft.com/
en-us/azure/architecture/gcp-professional/services
■ AWS to Azure services comparison https://learn.microsoft.com/en-us/
azure/architecture/aws-professional/services

It's important to note that having templated architectures that can accelerate the development of your solution can be a good litmus test for selecting
your cloud partner. As an example, both AWS and Azure have published
architectures on remote patient monitoring, and the links are included in the
resource section of this chapter.

Finally, ask yourself these questions when evaluating cloud vendors:

■ Which cloud do your target customers use?

- Are they operating in the regions you plan to target?
- Do you have special technical needs, like Large Language Models (LLMs) or Graphics Processing Unit (GPUs)?
- Will they mine your data?
- Will they have access to your IP?
- Are they likely to adopt or cannibalize your business model?
- What is the partner landscape for each cloud vendor and where could you plug in?
- Do you have colleagues or friends at the cloud provider who can be a champion for your solution and help you navigate these large, complex tech companies?
- What level of tech, sales, and Go to Market (GTM) support will you get?

And here are a few questions you should strike from your evaluation:

- Are they likely to purchase your company?
- How many cloud credits do they offer (while somewhat important, this by itself is not a reason to select a cloud, although many founders do, unfortunately)?

I specifically call these two questions out because I hear them frequently from founders, but they should not be part of the cloud selection criteria. It is everyone's dream to have a company like AWS buy them, but it rarely happens – really rarely. While this is across all industry segments, you can see how few AI startups each of the big tech companies acquire, in Figure 4.3, from CB Insights.

Other Options

If you are a non-technical founder, you may opt to select a development partner that can also provide cloud services. Being in the Microsoft ecosystem, I'm most familiar with 3Bcloud, (https://3cloudsolutions.com/), 2022 Microsoft Partner of the Year. Not only can they provide your company with Azure, but they can help you design and develop your solution.

Even if you are a technical founder, you may opt to accelerate your development by engaging with a systems integrator (SI) partner that has cloud experts. When asked, I typically share a list of about eight SI companies for startups to evaluate. This list of potential SI partners includes large, global

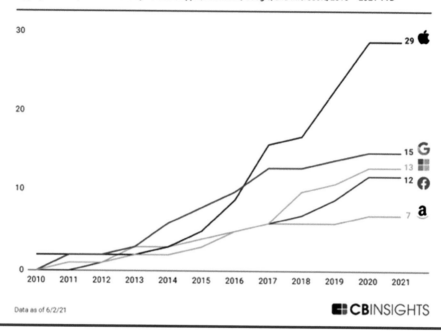

APPLE LEADS THE BIG TECH RACE FOR AI

Aggregate AI acquisitions made by Amazon, Apple, Facebook, Google, and Microsoft, 2010 – 2021 YTD

Data as of 6/2/21

Figure 4.3   Big tech make few acquisitions.

Source: The Race for AI: Which Tech Giants Are Snapping up Artificial Intelligence Startups (cbinsights
.com) https://www.cbinsights.com/reports/CB-Insights_Tech-Giants-Artificial-Intelligence.pdf?

organizations as well as smaller, boutique companies. Larger companies
also have the potential to be distribution channels for your startup, leverag-
ing their existing customers for your benefit (more on that in Chapter 9).
Conversely, they may see your solution as something they want to replicate
or acquire, so proper vetting and legal protections will be key. These SI
partners have both technology skills and industry expertise:

1. 3Cloud
2. Cognizant
3. HCL Technologies
4. Insight
5. Kepler Team
6. Logic 2020
7. Neudesic
8. Sonata Software
9. Tata Consultancy Services

It's critical that when selecting an SI partner, not only do the prices and terms need to fit, but there also needs to be a cultural fit to avoid conflicts by mismatched communications or approaches. Whether you opt for a 3BCloud type of company or a systems integration company, the single most important factor leading to a successful partnership and product is to have a leader on your team who is technically knowledgeable. This technical leader doesn't have to be a full-time employee; he or she can be a fractional CIO or CTO or an advisor or board member. The key is to make sure that this person has fully understood and can communicate your requirements for the solution you are building. Give them decision-making authority and have frequent (weekly, at a minimum) meetings to ensure everything and everyone is moving in the right direction. I have seen startups, without the right technical leadership, experience extreme delays in their product development, causing subsequent issues with compliance, funding, and business development activities.

In one case, by the time the $300K budget for the product development contract was spent, the startup was miles away from where the founders thought it would be. The founding team had delegated responsibility to the SI partner and, through a lack of communications and proper oversight, the system that was delivered wasn't customer ready. To be clear, *no one* was happy with how the relationship ended. The founding team had only a fraction of their solution ready for the market, and the SI partner had a very unhappy customer. With proper planning, communications, and consistent technical supervision, the solution might have been delivered as planned and the startup could have entered the market on schedule.

Interoperability

As mentioned in Chapter 2, point solution fatigue is an issue for companies that don't have products that are interoperable with standard healthcare systems and protocols (A point solution "addresses a single functional need within your [customer's] company").[15] Point solutions are easier to build, which is why we have so many in the market. However, they are harder to sell. Imagine having to log into each app on your cellphone, every time you wanted to use them. Or imagine that the email on your phone didn't synchronize with the email on your laptop or tablet. That would be annoying, right? Then why would you build a product that essentially requires your customers to do the same thing?

Clinicians, staff, scientists, and researchers are already overwhelmed by the number of portals, apps, and other electronic tools. Most don't want to add another system to log into, no matter how insightful or helpful the information may be. In healthcare and life sciences, there are specific protocols for data like FHIR (Fast Healthcare Interoperability Resources) and DICOM (Digital Imaging and Communications in Medicine).

■ **FHIR** – Microsoft notes that,

> With FHIR, organizations can unify disparate electronic health record systems (EHRs) and other health data repositories – allowing all data to be persisted and exchanged in a single, universal format. With the addition of SMART on FHIR, user-facing mobile and web-based applications can securely interact with FHIR data – opening a new range of possibilities for patient and provider access to PHI. Most of all, FHIR simplifies the process of assembling large health datasets for research – enabling researchers and clinicians to apply machine learning and analytics at scale for gaining new health insights.[16]

■ **DICOM** – UCSF states that DICOM is

> the international standard to transmit, store, retrieve, print, process, and display medical imaging information (source: https://www.dicomstandard.org/). Data is available in the DICOM format as produced by the imaging device. Each DICOM file contains extensive metadata in a header as well as pixel data for the image itself.[17]

As you would expect, the major cloud vendors have tools that enable data exchange and interoperability using these standards. Frankly, it doesn't matter which tool you use; it's just important to use them to make your solution interoperable and not another point solution. Remember the comment from the CIO I spoke with and shared in the preface? (If you didn't read it, the punchline is this: he had thousands of apps for his clinicians, and only a fraction of them were ever used. I suspect the small number of apps that are used are interoperable and seamlessly integrated into existing workflows.)

Additionally, if you are in the United States or targeting customers in the United States, you will want to monitor the developments around the Trusted Exchange Framework and Common Agreement (TEFCA).

TEFCA establishes a universal policy and technical floor for nation-wide interoperability; simplifies connectivity for organizations to securely exchange information to improve patient care, enhance the welfare of populations, and generate health care value; and enables individuals to gather their healthcare information. The Common Agreement establishes the infrastructure model and the governing approach for users in different networks to securely share basic clinical information under commonly agreed-to expectations and rules.[18]

Reuse of Technology

As you build your product development roadmap and technical architecture, consider how the technology might be reused to build additional products for your customers. Going back to the remote patient monitoring scenario, Sensoria Health (https://www.sensoriahealth.com/) has developed a remote patient monitoring (RPM) platform, based on a single technology architecture. Using the Sensoria Core, Microsoft Azure, and technical expertise, they have several RPM solutions in market including:

- **A diabetic foot wound boot** – To avoid amputations and promote healing
- **Wheelchair cushion** – To avoid pressure wounds for wheelchair users
- **Smart onesie** – To help monitor babies' key biometrics while they sleep
- **Smart sock** – To perform high-fidelity gait analysis[19]

Summary

Pitfall	Best Practice
You select a cloud vendor because your first technical hire knows that tool set	Fully evaluate your technology options • Select a cloud vendor that best fits your objectives • Carefully select outside partners, if needed • Have an in-house technical leader to guide development, even if only on a fractional basis

Resources

- AWS for Health | Healthcare & Life Sciences | AWS (amazon.com).
- Healthcare & Life Sciences | Google Cloud.

- Microsoft Cloud for Healthcare | Microsoft.
- What Is HL7 FHIR? (healthit.gov).
- About Health Level Seven International | HL7 International.
- Remote Patient Monitoring – Azure Architecture Center (https://learn .microsoft.com/en-us/azure/architecture/example-scenario/digital-health/ remote-patient-monitoring).
- Building IoMT Solutions to Accelerate Patient Outcomes on the AWS Cloud (https://aws.amazon.com/blogs/industries/building-iomt-solutions -to-accelerate-patient-outcomes-on-the-aws-cloud/).

Notes

1. Amazon Completes One Medical Takeover after FTC Nod, Discounts Membership | Reuters.
2. Amazon's Accelerator Is Working with 23 Startups to Help Address Healthcare Burnout (forbes.com).
3. How Amazon Makes Money: Shopping, Advertising, and Cloud – Investopedia. https://www.investopedia.com/how-amazon-makes-money-4587523.
4. Amazon Revenue, Amazon Sales and Amazon Profits – Digital Commerce 360. https://www.digitalcommerce360.com/article/amazon-sales/.
5. Amazon Reveals Its Most Profitable Business – Forbes. https://www.forbes.com /sites/jasongoldberg/2022/02/04/amazon-reveals-its-most-profitable-business/.
6. What We Get So Very Wrong about Amazon's Retail Profitability (forbes.com).
7. Amazon Reveals Its Most Profitable Business (forbes.com).
8. https://www.statista.com/statistics/633651/alphabet-annual-global-revenue-by -segment/.
9. https://www.cnbc.com/2021/05/18/how-does-google-make-money-advertising -business-breakdown-.html.
10. How Google (Alphabet) Makes Money: Advertising and Cloud – Investopedia. https://www.investopedia.com/articles/investing/020515/business-google.asp.
11. Microsoft Cloud for Healthcare | Avanade US.
12. How Microsoft Makes Money: Computing and Cloud Services – Investopedia. https://www.investopedia.com/how-microsoft-makes-money-4798809.
13. Microsoft Revenue Breakdown by Product, Segment and Country. https://www .kamilfranek.com/microsoft-revenue-breakdown/.
14. https://www.microsoft.com/investor/reports/ar22.
15. Point Solutions or an Integrated Platform: A Business-Critical Decision (forbes.com).
16. What Is the FHIR Service in Azure Health Data Services? | Microsoft Learn.
17. Imaging Data 101 | UCSF Radiology.
18. Interoperability | HealthIT.gov.
19. Sensoria Health.

Chapter 5

The Funds

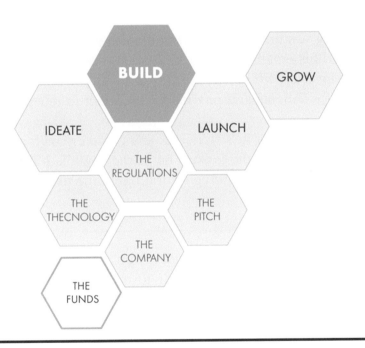

Figure 5.1   The funds.

Source: © Sally Ann Frank

> *I don't want to take on funding and dilute my ownership. I'll just bootstrap.*

Seeing a startup fail is painful. Most of the time, the reasons for the failure are clear – but unfortunately, not always to the founder. We are all familiar with the mega failures in digital health startups, the most notable one being Theranos. The healthcare equivalent of a Ponzi scheme, that particular failure

DOI: 10.4324/9781032639468-5

was due to a lack of ethics and the layers of lies that ensued. Thankfully, most founders who fail don't end up on the evening news or in prison. But while failure is painful, it can also be a tremendous learning experience.

I was advising a founder on his startup when I learned of his previous startup attempt. He was quick to admit that the first time around, he had no idea what he was doing. He had developed a medication adherence app that was designed to remind patients to take their medications consistently. This founder designed the entire app by himself, with no input from outsiders (except his parents who took medications daily and thought everything their son did was brilliant!). Furthermore, as a younger founder, he had no personal experience with a daily medication regimen. He didn't have a clear vision of what was helpful and what wasn't. No market research, customer discovery, or competitive analysis was conducted. He had an idea and started building.

Once the app was developed, he put together an investment deck and started contacting venture funds to drum up interest and funds. No one bit. No one returned his emails or phone calls. Until one day, he received an email from an investor, who told him the hard truth: the app was "crap," and had little value for patients and providers. Ouch. But in retrospect, it was a good ouch.

I'm happy to report that he's started a new company with a completely different solution, applying the lessons he learned. While it's still early, he is taking the time to do the right things at the right time to improve the likelihood of success.

Unless you are a successful, serial founder, with a track record of successful exits, bootstrapping is a bad idea. Finding investors is difficult, very difficult, but the process requires you to be incredibly disciplined about how you build your business. Bootstrapping is the opposite of disciplined development. With no one to answer to, it's possible that you might lose focus, over plan or under plan, over engineer or under engineer, or build go-to-market strategies that fall short. Summarizing from Investopedia,[1] Figure 5.2 provides a quick look at the pros and cons of venture capital.

The other key aspect to remember about a potential funding organization is that their mission is significantly different than yours. As a digital health founder, you are trying to solve a problem that is important to you, that will improve the lives and health of people – and you are eager to make money along the way. However, your VC friends, while bought into your mission, are more interested in a solid return on their investment. This means that you will be customer- or patient-focused, while they will be balance-sheet

Pros	Cons
• Provides early-stage companies with cash to fund operations • Offers a path to funding without the need to have cash flow or assets to secure VC funding • Includes (usually) VC-backed mentoring and networking services to help new companies secure talent and grow	• Demands a large share of company equity • Opens the door to losing creative control as investors demand immediate quick return on their investment (ROI) • Ferments pressure from VC for founders to exit rather than pursue long-term growth

Figure 5.2   Pros and cons of venture capital.

Source: © Sally Ann Frank

focused. This yin-yang relationship can be fraught with dissension, or it can be the balance that founders, especially first-time founders, need most.

Funding Basics

It's best if you think of potential funding partners as potential spouses, and your relationship with them is like a marriage. It is likely that you will do everything together, especially for your lead investor. But before we marry you off, let's start with some basic terms about the types of funding sources:

- **Angel investor** – Invests in you and your idea. Typically, an angel investor is, "a high-net-worth individual who provides financial backing for small startups and entrepreneurs typically in exchange for equity."[2] Angels can invest on an ongoing basis or may opt to invest only one time. Often, they do not require a lot of due diligence up front, as they are betting on you and your idea, and are willing to shoulder the risk of the funds they have invested.
- **Lead investor** – Initiates the venture capital in a financial arrangement. Usually, the lead investor has the highest share of the capital that will be given as a support to a fund-raising company. However, in some cases, the lead investor might not be the highest shareholder but just an investor agreed upon by the group of investors to lead and represent their interest in the financial arrangement.[3]
- **Strategic (or corporate) investor** – Makes venture investments, providing not only capital, but also guidance on the product roadmap, engineering and development resources, and critical introductions. Strategic investors are also known as corporate venture capital firms, like Microsoft's M12.[4]

■ **Venture capital (or institutional) investor** – Invests in exchange
  for equity, with an eye toward a big return on their investment at
  some future date. There are lots of these types of companies, from
  the big ones like Andreessen Horovitz, to healthcare specific funds,
  like OrbiMed, to smaller, niche investors, like WXR Fund, which,
  "invests in two of the greatest opportunities of our time: spatial computing + female entrepreneurs."[5] VC companies will also take an active
  interest in your startup like strategic investors, and may have represen-
  tation on your board, as an advisor or observer. While they are there
  to help you, their priority is to protect and generate returns on their
  investments.

EY provides helpful details on the differences between corporate (or strategic) venture companies and traditional VCs. They highlight the similarities
in activities and processes: (1) source opportunities, (2) perform diligence
to evaluate their attractiveness, (3) negotiate and execute transactions, (4)
manage the resulting portfolio of investments and (5) guide them through
the process of achieving liquidity.[6] The article goes on to explain the key
areas of differences between CVCs and VCs including: (1) investor base, (2)
Limited Partner (LP) engagement, (3) investment horizon, (4) management
structure, (5) motivations, (6) behavioral drivers, and (7) approach to adding
value.

Regardless of what type of funding you pursue, during your discussions and negotiations, you should learn their answers to the seven areas
above. It can be a litmus test to make sure that you and your investor are in
alignment.

Additionally, the moment you have a business plan, and before you
need funding, begin researching potential funding sources. Select a few
VC firms that you think may be good options for you and follow them
on social media to see if their investment style, theses, and culture are a
potential fit. Ideally, you want to start building relationships with potential
funders before you seek investment. As mentioned previously, the relationship with your investors will be like a marriage, and similarly, you will
want to get to know them (and they you) before diving into a business
relationship.

Funding Types

There are lots of ways to fund your company. To help sort through the
options, Figure 5.3 is a brief overview of the pros and cons of each type.

Type of funding	Pros	Cons
Angel – less formal funding process which includes exchanging money for equity, usually a high-wealth individual	Easier to execute, can be one time infusion or ongoing support	Not suitable for scaling but is better suited for early-stage companies, building their plans and MVPs
Venture Capital (either corporate or institutional) – more formal process where a company invests	More complex, but usually comes with additional support and possibly a board member, advisor or observer, which can be helpful, especially for first-time founders	More complex and can add people to your management team that you may not want to have undue influence, especially for serial entrepreneurs
Simple Agreement for Future Equity (SAFE) – a promise of equity at a future date	Easier to execute and well-suited for very early-stage companies	Usually are small amounts and are not suitable for scale, but are better suited for funding market research, prototypes and MVPs

Figure 5.3   Overview of types of venture capital.

Source: © Sally Ann Frank

Stage is also a key element of your funding strategy. As you build your business plan, you also need to consider when you will need infusions of capital to fund your company and build your solution. While there are no fixed rules, Figure 5.4 is an overview of funding types, mapped to the stage of your company and regulatory journey.

Funding Type	Stage(s) to seek this type of funding	Regulatory stage
Pre-seed/Angel/SAFE	Ideation, business planning, market research, prototyping	Being researched
Seed	MVP, product-market-fit (seed funding for PMF is especially common in healthcare and life sciences)	Filed for approval
Series A	PMF and ready to scale	Regulatory approval
Series B	Post PMF, continuing to scale and expand solution features or build adjacent solutions	Regulatory approval

Figure 5.4   Funding type mapped to stages.

Source: © Sally Ann Frank

If you are a minority founder, you are keenly aware of the additional barriers to funding that you may be encountering. "Only about 1.87% of $31 billion held by 200 venture capital funds has been allocated to startups with diverse leaders, according to a report from the nonprofit Diversity VC."[7] Therefore, you should research the growing number of funds and VC firms that are eager to invest in companies like yours. Here are a few examples:

- **WXR Fund** (https://www.wxrfund.com/) invests in spatial computing companies founded by female founders
- **Elevate Capital** (https://elevate.vc/), is the nation's first institutional venture capital fund that specifically targets investments in underserved entrepreneurs—such as women and ethnic minorities, or those with limited access regionally to capital and opportunities. We support visionaries with disruptive ideas and products through two specialized investment vehicles.[8]
- **Echo VC** (https://www.echovc.com/), specializes in "unapologetically investing in women, underrepresented founders (particularly of African descent) and underserved POC markets, backing bold ideas and business models that harness the power of technology to deliver value to mass markets."[9]
- **Serena Ventures** (https://www.serenaventures.com/), established by Serena Williams, outlines their investment thesis this way, "Through a champion mindset and unparalleled network, we empower founders to change the world."[10]
- **JumpStart Nova** (https://jumpstartnova.com/), with a mission to, dedicating ourselves to a group of chronically overlooked founders who we know, when given the opportunity, will make the healthcare industry better. Some of these founders will focus on solving the problems that lead to significant health inequities; while others will bring solutions to the market that will improve the entire industry.[11]
- **Goddess Gaia Ventures** (https://www.ggventures.co.uk/), describes themselves this way, Goddess Gaia Ventures is a female founded venture capital firm. We are building a £100 Mln venture fund that will invest in tech, products and solutions that cater towards the service of women's healthcare needs in Health, Wellness and Femtech. Our investments are aligned with creating a sustainable, healthy planet and society.[12]
- **The Global Good Fund** (https://globalgoodfund.org/global-impact-fund-ii/) is a $10M venture capital fund that invests in companies led by social entrepreneurs with a preference for companies led by people of color and women. GIF II's impact focus is primarily in environmental sustainability, health and health care, education, financial technology, socioeconomic mobility, and income equality, although GIF II is also permitted to make investments in other sectors.[13]

Lastly, if you are in the United States, don't forget to investigate additional funding that may be available through the Small Business Innovation Research (SBIR) and the Small Business Technology Transfer (STTR) grant programs (https://www.sbir.gov/) or your state government. For example, Maryland has a robust set of programs (that include funding and grants) for startups, which are outlined on the state website at https://business.maryland .gov/resources/funding-programs.

Now that we've gone through the types of funders and funding, let's cover the minimum artifacts that you need on your funding journey, namely, a data room, pitch deck, and historical profit and loss (P&L) and burn rate.

Data Room

A data room is a secure location for startups to share their confidential information with prospective investors. At a minimum, the data room includes information about your company and its projected growth, including your pitch deck, cap table, and historical P&L and burn[14]. It has two primary benefits:

1. **Internal discipline** – Putting together all the information for a winning data room takes time and an eye for financial detail. It also requires you to look at your business from an outsider's perspective – if you were considering investing in your company, what information would you want to have?
2. **Due diligence** – Investors typically review the artifacts in the data room as part of their evaluation process. Through the documentation you provide, they will begin to assess their risk and potential gains from investing in your company.

What goes into a data room? This list from Andreessen Horowitz is a great starting point for SaaS solutions:

- Monthly active free users and paid subscribers
- Monthly recurring revenue (MRR) and gross margin
- Conversion rates for each step in the flow: install to registration to trial to paying user

- Acquisition split between organic and paid users monthly, and paid CAC [Customer Acquisition Cost]
- % of users on each type of plan (e.g., monthly vs. annual)
- Monthly retention cohorts — paid user retention (% of users still paying for a subscription at X month), and active user retention (% of users still using the app at X month)[15]

Let's dig in deeper into the basic elements of a data room, the pitch deck, cap table, and historical P&L and burn rates.

Investor Pitch Deck

Let's start by clarifying that your investor pitch deck is different from your pitch deck. While there are common elements, there are parts of your investor deck that are not suitable for prospective customers. The customer pitch deck will be covered in Chapter 7 – The Pitch.

As for investor pitch decks, there are plenty of examples online, like this one, Sample Investor Pitch Deck for a Startup (AllBusiness.com https://www.allbusiness.com/sample-investor-pitch-deck-startup-110753-1.html). Many sources quibble about the correct length of a pitch deck for investors, but I think ten is the right number, and Guy Kawasaki, the legendary business author and entrepreneur, agrees. In fact, his 10/20/30 rule is still valid today, though the concept was shared in a 2015 article that he wrote.[16] In short, Guy stipulates that your investor pitch deck should have 10 slides, take 20 minutes to present, and be in 30-point font. You can even check out his template and download it here: https://www.canva.com/design/DAEhUeYe_fo/view.

Guy is a smart guy and has been doing this for a while, so I won't refute his approach. However, I would change a few things, and I've included some examples that I really like. Please note that these slides are from actual companies (except the title page). Aesthetically, these may not follow Guy's 30-point font rule and may fly in the face of good design, but in this setting, function prevails over form.

Title Page

Interestingly, I couldn't find a single pitch deck with all the elements that I think are important. Specifically, it should have the name and logo of your

Figure 5.5   Mockup of title slide.

Source: © Sally Ann Frank

company, and your name, title, and contact information. Figure 5.5 is a quick mockup.

The Ask

Most people put the slide with the request for funding at the end of the deck. I like to move it up to the front, so that as the investor is listening to the pitch, he or she can have the end in mind, just like you probably do. Whether I'm drafting an email or presentation deck or any artifact that will include a request, I always start with the request. My father drilled it into me, "Ask for what you want first, and keep the end in mind for all involved." This advice works well in venture funding, too. I particularly like this slide from Infinadeck, shown in Figure 5.6, because it is clear what they are seeking in funding, what they will use the funds for, and how much funding they have already received and from where.

The Problem

This AEYE Health slide in Figure 5.7 does a great job of showing, with high impact graphics, the extent of the problem they are trying to solve. I especially like how they take the number of diabetes patients in both the US market and globally. Then they go one step further to show the number of patients not being screened for diabetic retinopathy. The only thing I would

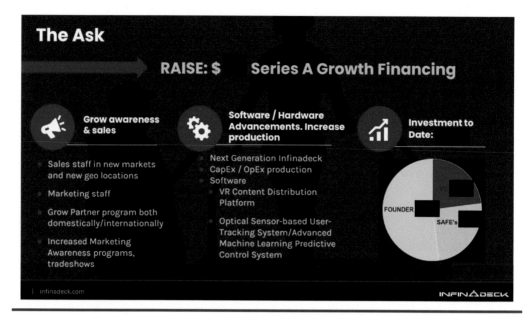

Figure 5.6   **The ask.**

Source: Investor Deck, Infinadeck, Ken Bossung

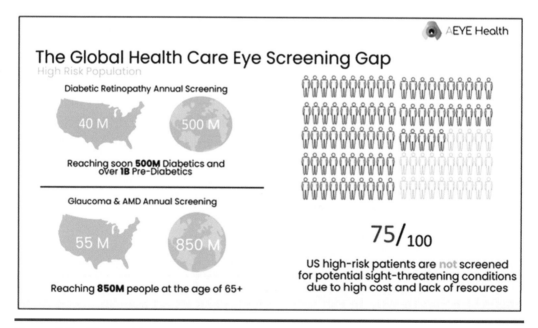

Figure 5.7   **The problem.**

Source: Investor Deck, AEYE Health, Zack Dvey-Aharon, PhD.

change here is to add a citation and source for their data. While I'm fairly certain these numbers are on track, citing an authoritative source brings credibility to these numbers and the pitch.

The Value Proposition

The value proposition can be very tricky to convey, as you want to be measured in the claims you make about your solution. Over the top, "the best thing since sliced bread," won't work. But you also don't want to be too humble in your approach either – getting funding is probably the most competitive business process ever. Striking the right balance between bravado and bashfulness is key. Pangaea Data does a terrific job (Figure 5.8) striking exactly the right balance, as they showcase their value proposition through the lens of existing customers, with quantitative results to back up their approach.

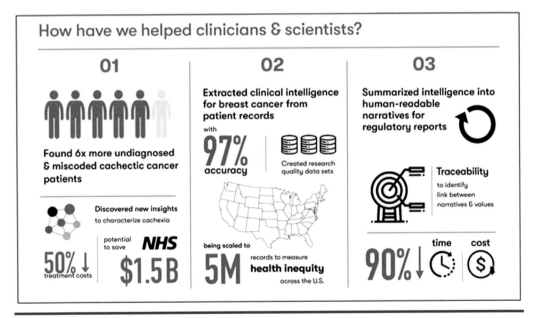

Figure 5.8   The value proposition.

Source: Investor Deck, Pangaea Data, Vibhor Gupta

The Management Team

Investors take the management team very seriously. From what I have been told, investors are more likely to select a killer management team with an average solution than an average management team with a killer solution. So, keep that in mind, both when hiring and when pitching your company. (More on key hires in Chapter 6.) Michael Greeley, General Partner at Flare Capital stresses the "importance of the extended team: relevance, experience, understanding, 'voice of the customer,' etc. – super critical. Great people always attract capital."[17] It's important to share the background of your key team members without overstating or seeming arrogant. In Figure 5.9, from Integrate.ai, in one slide they share who their key leaders are, note prominent companies they worked for, and include accolades and regulatory standing all in one handy slide. When information can be presented like this, getting to a ten-page slide deck is achievable.

Figure 5.9   The management team.

Source: Investor Deck, integrate.ai, Steve Irvine

The Competitive Advantage

Declaring your competitive advantage isn't always easy. There may be other entrants in the market that seem to be like your solution, even though you know it's different and superior (in your eyes, of course). For example, Hyro is a conversational AI company, which is a fairly crowded segment, even within healthcare and life sciences. However, they do a tremendous job with their messaging, especially when it comes to their "secret sauce" (I also love their marketing and messaging. I encourage you to follow them on LinkedIn, just to see how innovative they are with their go-to-market strategy). In Figure 5.10, they both quickly and clearly convey how they are different. (They also have a tremendous track record with their customers, but I'll touch on that later in Chapter 7.)

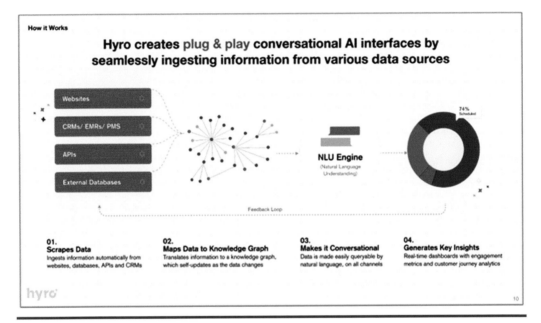

Figure 5.10   The competitive advantage.

Source: Investor Deck, Hyro, Aaron Bours

The Competitive Analysis

Like TAM, competitive analyses can also be viewed with a skeptical eye by investors. Often, the analysis isn't thorough or does not consider all the possible competitors. Additionally, any competitive analysis that also doesn't show where you are weak, is probably not a complete analysis. Figure 5.11 from Vital Start, is an easy-to-read table that I like very much; it's straightforward and doesn't take a lot of time to understand. However, defining the column headings would be helpful (or adding a few descriptive words). While the format is helpful and used widely, many startups fail to show where they lag behind their competitors. Are they that far ahead or is the analysis flawed? That is for you to consider, even though the format is terrific.

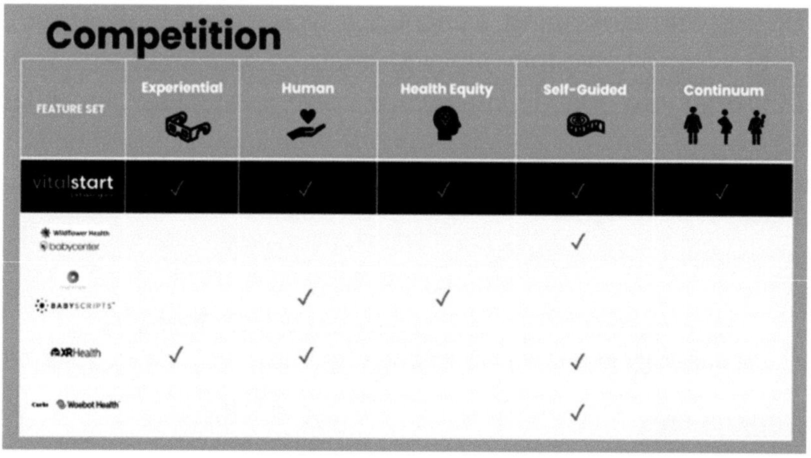

Figure 5.11 **The competitive analysis.**

Source: Investor Deck, Vital Start Health, Kirthika Parmeswaran

Business Model

I have seen several startups fall flat with their business models. By the time you are putting an investor deck together, you should know how you will get paid, what your wedge offer is, and how you will move your customers from proof of concepts (POCs) to pilot projects to full blown implementation. We will go into more depth about the business model in Chapter 9 - The GTM strategy, but for your investor deck, you should have a single slide that outlines your business model. In the fictional scenario below (because no startup wants me to broadcast their business model), I've outlined three tiers that make up the business model for this fake SaaS company in Figure 5.12. I've also added logos for the fake customers. In a real investor deck, you may list existing customers and add those that are in the pipeline if you think there is better than a 50% chance of closing the deal. Those investors will remember every customer that you list, so be judicious about who you include.

The Go-to-Market Plan

Like the business model, I don't feel comfortable sharing an actual go-to-market plan, although we will dive into more detail in Chapter 10. For the single slide encapsulating your GTM plan, it should have some key elements, including a timeline and market segments, and I've even seen some

BUSINESS MODEL

Freemium

- Introductory level
- Limited features
- Limited transactions or compute
- On-ramp for greater consumption

Starter

- Additonal features
- Price per transaction or compute
- On-ramp for enterprise license

Enterprise

- Site license
- Unlimited users or transactions
- Improved per unit pricing as usage grows

Customer (fictitious logos)

Figure 5.12   The business model.

Source: © Sally Ann Frank

with projections of break-even points and additional funding rounds. Again, building something that is fictitious, Figure 5.13 shows some of the elements that you can include in your GTM slide.

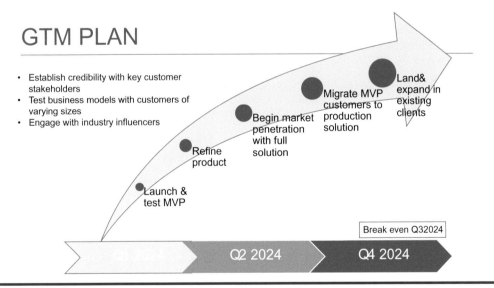

Figure 5.13   GTM plan.

Source: © Sally Ann Frank

The Financials and Metrics

For spreadsheet jockeys, this can be the most straightforward part of the investor deck. Basically, you can just copy and paste your financial projections into a slide. I particularly like the format in Figure 5.14, used by a few of the startups that I know. It's high level but provides all the details for the first meeting with investors.

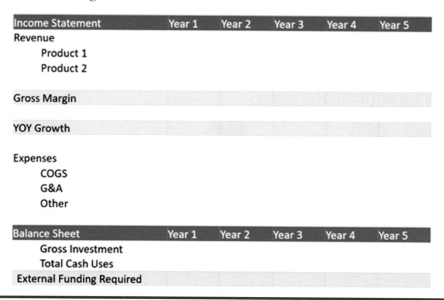

Figure 5.14 The financial projections.

Source: © Sally Ann Frank

The Progress to Date

This may be the most difficult topic to put on a single slide. Often there is SO much you want to cover to convince your prospective investor that you are legit and worth the risk. I like the approach from Wellness Wits in Figure 5.15, as it includes a timeline, key milestones, and critical path activities. I also recommend that this slide conveys your regulatory status, if you need FDA, CE, or other approvals and pinpoints when you think that process will be completed.

As you build your investor pitch, there are a few topics you want to treat delicately:

■ **Total addressable market (TAM)** is a term that is often bandied about to show the impact that a startup can have on a specific business segment. In my view, TAM is often meaningless, especially when coupled with some astronomical number representing the future market share that a tiny company expects to capture. Furthermore, many investors will do their own TAM calculations, so be careful when discussing

Our path to growth: Strategic Partnerships to expand our virtual care teams and user base in 2023

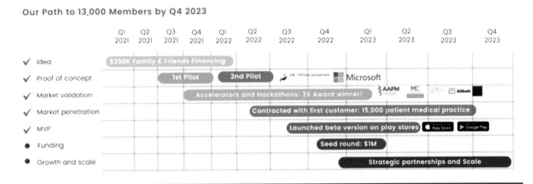

Figure 5.15   The progress to date.

Source: Investor Deck, Wellness Wits, Kike Oduba, MD, MPH, CIC, NB-HWC

TAM and don't inflate the numbers or your ability to capture a huge segment of the market.

■ **Revenue**, especially future revenue, is likely a guess, albeit an educated one. The salesperson in you is likely to overstate, while the engineer in you is likely to understate. Whichever way you lean, find the right balance and come up with a reasonable revenue forecasting model that generates numbers you both like.

■ **Regulatory path** can be fraught with delays, uncertainties, and changes in policies. Be as realistic as you can, balancing both the most pessimistic and optimistic approaches to find the right estimate. If you want to get an understanding of the backlog on regulatory approval, ask your legal team. And if you are really curious, you can go to Device Approvals, Denials and Clearances | FDA (https://www.fda.gov/medical-devices/products-and-medical-procedures/device-approvals-denials -and-clearances) and drill down into one of the approvals and you can see how long it takes. For example, Sonavi Labs is the startup with an industry-leading digital stethoscope that I mentioned in Chapter 3. They applied for their 510(k) approval in March of 2020, and received approval in September 2020.[18] That is very fast (but don't get your hopes up!), but the database is helpful to understand the process.

Lastly, before leaving the topic of your investor pitch deck, consider this segment from the podcast, All-In (All-In Podcast – YouTube, https://www.

youtube.com/@allin). In their 13 June 2023 episode (https://youtu.be /5cQXjboJwg0?t=3722) they talk about the value of the written word, in contrast to only using PowerPoint decks. Investor Chamath Palihapitiya, talks about the pitfalls of decks and how narrative is better for truly grasping concepts. He says:

> *I've been writing for years… it allows you to actually find people who will critique things in a thoughtful, intelligent way. It's hard to critique decks because you use broken English, you use fancy graphics. All of a sudden, somebody that's very good at graphical layout can dupe somebody else and so you don't get to good outcomes because this weird groupthink effect sets in when you look at decks.* **So, I'm not a fan of decks. I use them, but they need to be a companion to some sort of long form narrative document and I just think it's more useful.** *You get people who can really think about what they agree about, what they don't agree about. It shows the intellect of the person writing it quite honestly. Decks are very dangerous, I think. If you're gonna make decisions, I would encourage you, the bigger the decision, the deck is insufficient. It can be a companion piece but it needs to be attached along with documents.*

With this in mind, you may want to consider adding a document to your data room that fills in the gaps mentioned by Chamath. Imagine that you are an investor, and you open a data room to find a document that explains the company, the deal, and all the details you need for your analysis – in a form that you can easily add to your investment memo. Your interest and affinity for the company increases on the spot. If you've never seen an investment memo, Bessemer Venture Partners have some of their investment memos on their website (https://www.bvp.com/memos), showing what it takes to get Bessemer Venture Partners to invest in you. This is a tremendous resource to learn how VCs think and evaluate investment options.

Cap Table

A capitalization or cap table is basically a spreadsheet showing who has equity in the company. While that sounds straightforward, the complexity of the cap table is directly related to how many investors you have and the types of equity they hold. According to Investopedia:

- A capitalization table is a table showing the equity ownership capitalization for a company.
- The capitalization table is essential for financial decisions involving equity ownership, market capitalization, and market value.
- Capitalization tables help private companies maintain the calculation of their market value. In the private market, they are also important for shareholder reporting and new capital issuance marketing.[19]

Often employees may have equity options for the future, while angel or seed investors own equity in exchange for their funds. This is one of the many reasons that serious founders, and especially those in healthcare and life sciences, are not keen on crowdfunding. It can be done, but no one wants to keep track of those who invest $100 here or $500 there. The fewer entities in your cap table, the easier it is to manage that part of your business.

Carta (www.carta.com) does a terrific job explaining cap tables and even offers a free, online course that outlines the basics (Cap table 101 – Section 1 | Carta Classroom, https://carta.com/learn/cap-table-101/1/?ir=blog-cap-table-hero1&slide=1). Keep in mind that you, as the founder or member of the founding team, need to understand and monitor your cap table. Ideally, however, you will employ a trained professional to manage this part of your business. This is not a full-time job, so a fractional expert may be the right choice for you.

Historical P&L and Burn

According to Andreessen Horowitz, this part of the data room shows the path from gross revenue through net income (loss) through cash outflow monthly. They advise founders to break out different types of revenue (if applicable) and all major costs. It's also helpful to add your cash balance, if you're not including a balance sheet and cash flow statement.[20] They also provide this sample of what they expect to see that you may find helpful, shown in Figure 5.16.

Making It Real

While I meet hundreds of startups in my work, and advise some on their funding journey, I've never had the experience of raising funds myself. Therefore, I asked a friend, healthcare executive, and serial entrepreneur,

Historical P&L and Burn

	Jan-22	Feb-22	Mar-22	Apr-22	May-22	Jun-22	Jul-22
# of Bookings	1000	1200	1500	1600	1700	1750	2000
Average GBV	$250	$272	$301	$281	$290	$304	$311
GMV	$250,000	$326,400	$391,300	$421,500	$493,000	$532,000	$623,000
% MoM Change		31%	20%	8%	17%	8%	17%
Host Fees	$20,000	$26,112	$31,304	$33,720	$39,440	$42,560	$49,700
Guest Fees	$30,000	$39,168	$46,956	$50,580	$59,160	$63,840	$74,640
Net Revenue	$50,000	$65,280	$78,260	$84,300	$98,600	$106,400	$124,400
% MoM Change		31%	20%	8%	17%	8%	17%
Payment Processing Fees	$7,500	$9,792	$11,739	$12,645	$14,790	$15,960	$18,660
Supplier Vetting	$5,000	$5,500	$6,000	$7,000	$7,700	$8,200	$8,600
Customer Support & Ops	$2,000	$4,200	$4,700	$4,700	$4,900	$5,200	$6,500
COGS	$14,500	$19,492	$22,439	$24,345	$27,390	$29,360	$33,760
Gross Profit	$35,500	$45,788	$55,821	$59,955	$71,210	$77,040	$90,640
Gross Margin	71%	70%	71%	71%	72%	72%	73%
Variable Local Labor	$5,500	$6,200	$7,700	$8,500	$9,200	$9,900	$9,800
Marketing Expense	$10,000	$15,000	$15,000	$20,000	$20,000	$25,000	$25,000
Sales Commissions	$7,700	$8,200	$9,500	$10,200	$11,500	$13,200	$14,600
Indirect Variable Costs	$23,200	$29,400	$32,200	$38,700	$40,700	$48,100	$49,400
Contribution Profit	$12,300	$16,388	$23,621	$21,255	$30,510	$28,940	$41,240
Contribution Margin	25%	25%	30%	25%	31%	27%	33%
Compensation & Benefits	$89,500	$95,400	$100,500	$110,400	$125,000	$128,400	$145,000
Software	$5,000	$5,000	$7,500	$7,500	$9,000	$9,000	$9,000
Travel & Entertainment	$2,500	$3,000	$3,500	$3,500	$4,000	$4,200	$5,000
Facilities Expenses	$33,000	$33,000	$33,000	$33,000	$33,000	$33,000	$33,000
Other G&A	$800	$990	$1,000	$1,100	$1,200	$1,300	$1,250
Other Expenses	$130,800	$137,390	$145,500	$155,510	$172,200	$175,900	$193,250
EBITDA	-$118,500	-$121,002	-$121,879	-$134,255	-$141,690	-$146,960	-$152,010
Interest, Taxes, Depreciation (Net)	$0	$0	$0	$0	$0	$0	$0
Net Income	-$118,500	-$121,002	-$121,879	-$134,255	-$141,690	-$146,960	-$152,010
Ending Cash Balance	$10,000,000	$9,878,998	$9,757,119	$9,622,864	$9,481,174	$9,334,214	$9,182,204

Illustrative example for a marketplace startup

a16z Consumer

Figure 5.16   The historical P&L and burn rates.

Source: Data-Room_-Historical-PL-and-Burn.png (2000 × 2902) (wp.com), https://i0.wp.com/a16z.com/wp-content/uploads/2022/12/Data-Room_-Historical-PL-and-Burn.png?ssl=1

Lisa Maki, to share her experiences and observations with me. As co-founder and CEO of both PockitDok and BeliefNetworks, Inc. (both with successful exits), Lisa has first-hand knowledge of the fund-raising journey. Our conversation was rich with wisdom, guidance, and common sense (which often isn't so common). We recorded the call and had our AI tool capture the notes (slightly edited for clarity):

■ Lisa talked about the use of convertible and SAFE notes for early-stage funding. Both investment instruments have pros and cons and it's important for founders and investors to thoroughly understand the benefits and risks of the instrument they're using.
  – Lisa discussed the decision to structure her last startup's seed round as an institutional round, which took more work up front but streamlined the funding process moving forward and created transparency for both the company and investors. It's now possible to complete an equity round fairly inexpensively and it's worth considering.

■ Lisa talked about her experience raising funds for a healthcare startup and the difficulty of aligning an early-stage institutional venture with the long lead time often required to attain market fit in the healthcare industry. She discussed that founders may need to look to healthcare corporate investors to complete a round as well as provide valuable industry insights and introductions.
  – Lisa and Sally discussed the reasons attaining market fit takes longer and often costs more for a healthcare startup. For example, the length of a US healthcare enterprise sale can take 18–36 months, pushing the time to validation of market fit to four years or more.
  – Lisa and Sally discussed that the long sales cycle in the healthcare and life sciences industries is due to the aversion to high risk in a regulated industry.

■ Lisa and Sally discussed the differences and similarities between corporate venture funds and institutional venture funds. For example, while they both invest cash in exchange for equity, where they differ is that institutional funds invest on behalf of a diverse portfolio of limited partners – such as institutional investors and family desks – while corporate VCs typically invest on behalf of a single parent company.

■ They discussed the pros and cons of accepting lead investment from strategic investors. Lisa suggested that while both funds prioritize the success of the company as lead investors, a corporate investor's investment objectives may change with the changing business strategies of their parent company.

– Lisa and Sally discussed if there is a correlation between long-term success and being incubated and spun out of an organization like a provider or academic medical center (AMC). While she has not looked at the data, Lisa guessed that the mortality rate of companies incubated by providers is likely as great as those founded independently.

■ Lisa and Sally discussed the importance of investing in people rather than solutions. They agreed that an institutional investor will typically prioritize a great team, even if their initial idea is unvetted, over a mediocre team with an industry vetted solution. The road to market fit and profitability is long and there are no guarantees. Successful execution requires a resilient team with the ability to adapt and know when and how to course correct successfully. These are qualities you look for in an early-stage team, before financials and business models which will likely change.

Summary

Pitfall	Best Practice
Delaying or eschewing funding altogether	Consider options in relation to key milestones • What resources are needed to build an MVP? • How long will regulatory approval take? • Can I onboard customers with my current architecture and infrastructure? • If I can't get funding, are my idea and company still viable?

Resources

■ The Insider's Guide to Data Rooms: What to Know Before You Raise | Andreessen Horowitz (a16z.com).
■ VC 101: Key VC Terminology for Savvy Investors – Alumni Ventures.
■ Difference in institutional VCs and corporate VCs | EY – US.
■ "Hope Is Not a Business Model": Digital Health Fundraising Advice from 2 VCs – MedCity News.

Notes

1. Venture Capital: What Is VC and How Does It Work? (investopedia.com).
2. Angel Investor Definition and How It Works (investopedia.com).
3. Lead Investor (Venture Capital) – Explained – The Business Professor, LLC.
4. Should You Consider a Strategic Investor When Raising Venture Capital? – Crunchbase.
5. The WXR Fund.
6. Difference in Institutional VCs and Corporate VCs | EY – US.
7. Diversity VC Reports 1.87% of Venture Capital Allocated to Women and Minority-Owned Startups | VentureBeat.
8. The Inclusive Portland Venture Capital Firm | Elevate Capital.
9. EchoVC Partners4.
10. Serena Ventures – The Serena Williams-Backed VC Fund.
11. Jumpstart Nova – About.
12. https://www.ggventures.co.uk/.
13. Global Impact Fund II – THE GLOBAL GOOD FUND.
14. The Insider's Guide to Data Rooms: What to Know Before You Raise | Andreessen Horowitz (a16z.com).
15. The Insider's Guide to Data Rooms: What to Know Before You Raise | Andreessen Horowitz (a16z.com).
16. The Only 10 Slides You Need in Your Pitch – Guy Kawasaki.
17. Email exchange with Michael Greeley, July 29, 2023.
18. K200862.pdf (fda.gov).
19. Capitalization (Cap) Table: What It Is, Creating/Maintaining One (investopedia.com).
20. The Insider's Guide to Data Rooms: What to Know Before You Raise | Andreessen Horowitz (a16z.com).

Chapter 6

The Company

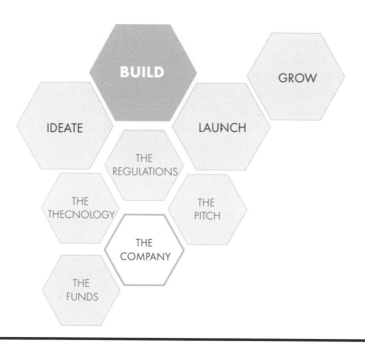

Figure 6.1   The company.

Source: © Sally Ann Frank

> *This company will be a trailblazer and wildly successful.*

A large financial services firm began building a healthcare specific solution which eventually spun out into a newco. They hired a leadership team, bought another startup, and launched their AI and data management company. It was an auspicious start for a new company, as this fledging company had a solution they could sell, funds for operations, a product

DOI: 10.4324/9781032639468-6

roadmap, and seasoned leadership. The consensus was that they were going to hit the market and grow exponentially and quickly.

However, it was not to be. Instead of looking at the market and responding to or anticipating market needs and trends, they began building a whole new ecosystem of solutions, partners, and collaborators. Essentially, they were trying to build a new industry – a challenging task for large companies, and even more difficult for small ones. Furthermore, there was a lack of focus on tactical activities to support the overall strategy. Meetings hashed through changes to, or refinements of, the big picture, and little time was spent on building the plans to achieve overall goals. Confidence in the company began to wane, causing several senior employees and advisors to recuse themselves from the startup.

Being a trailblazer and assuming you will be wildly successful is not the first thing that should come to mind. The first thing that should come to mind is your target customer and the problem you are trying to solve, which was covered in Chapter 2. I challenge you to separate your ego from your company. While it reflects you (and others who join you), personalities should be subordinate to the company mission. Put your customers at the center of every strategy and tactic, and the rest (revenue, reputation, and growth) will come. But let's start at the beginning.

The Company Structure

To reiterate, please seek legal advice from a trusted business attorney when structuring your company. I'm not providing legal advice; however, the legal firms listed in Chapter 3 *can* help. This overview in Figure 6.2 is merely educational, perhaps taking you back to your business 101 course from years ago.

Once you've selected your corporate structure, perhaps with some partners, it's time to start building the infrastructure of your company, namely your team, corporate identity, business model, and regulatory journey.

The Team and Tribe

I call this section, "the team and the tribe," because there are two primary stakeholders for you to consider: those who are part of the company as

Type	Features	Ownership	Liability	Taxes
Sole proprietor	Easy to establish Complete control Good while researching the market	One person	Unlimited personal liability	Self-employment tax Personal tax
Partnership	LP – one person has unlimited liability. LLP – limited liability to all partners	Two or more people	Unlimited personal liability unless structured as a limited partnership	Self-employment tax (except for limited partners) Personal tax
Limited Liability Corporation (LLC)	Best parts of corporations and partnerships Personal protection against liability Lower tax rate than corporations	One or more people	Owners are not personally liable	Self-employment tax Personal tax or corporate tax
C Corp	Separate from owners Strongest protection from personal liability Can raise money through stock offerings	One or more people	Owners are not personally liable	Corporate tax
S Corp	Avoids double taxation Profits/Losses can be pass through to owners personal taxation	One or more people but no more than 100, and all must be US citizens	Owners are not personally liable	Personal tax

Figure 6.2 The corporate structure.

Source: Summarized from: Choose a Business Structure | U.S. Small Business Administration (sba.gov) https://www.sba.gov/business-guide/launch-your-business/choose-business-structure

employees or partners (the team), and those who are supporting you along the way, without day-to-day responsibilities (the tribe).

The Team

Your founding team is the most important decision you will make, second only to the decision to start a company. From the outset, you want to think about key functions for which you want to hire and the channels you will use to find the right people. I cannot stress this next point enough: don't make easy hires. In other words, resist the temptation to hire your sister, cousin, best friend from high school, or some other person who is already a part of your social or family circle. If you look at the truly successful entrepreneurs, they seek people and opinions unlike their own. You are probably familiar with the many studies that show diverse boards generate better results.

> Companies with more culturally and ethnically diverse executive teams were 33% more likely to see better-than-average profits. In McKinsey's previous study—conducted with 2014 numbers—that increase had been 35%. At the board of directors' level, more ethnically and cultural diverse companies were 43% more likely to see above-average profits, showing a significant correlation between diversity and performance.[1]

Contrast those statistics with the possible issues in hiring a close friend or family member.

> An employee who is related to you might assume they have special privileges. They might try to abuse you and your business. At the same time, it's easy for you to take advantage of your relatives and set higher expectations for them. You might exploit them into working more or taking less pay.[2]

I'm not saying never work with close friends and family, but if you must, be strategic about it. For example, our friends at Sonavi Labs, founded by Ellington West, are commercializing technology patented by her father, James West, PhD.[3] Clearly, building a digital stethoscope using Dr West's patented technology is something they can do together. However, this type of arrangement is rare and very different from hiring your brother-in-law as your CTO.

If you are not going to hire friends and family, how do you find the right people to bring into the company? As a big LinkedIn fan and user (and not just because Microsoft owns it), I recommend combing through your contacts who have skills that you need, who also have mutual connections with you. For example, let's say I want to hire someone who has a healthcare background, talks about venture funding, and attended Stanford. Through filtering in LinkedIn, I found 17 people who fit, as shown in Figure 6.3.

And that is just the beginning. LinkedIn has tools for posting jobs or you can simply post that you are hiring, with specific details on the role. Just be prepared for lots and lots of inquiries, should you choose to go the posting

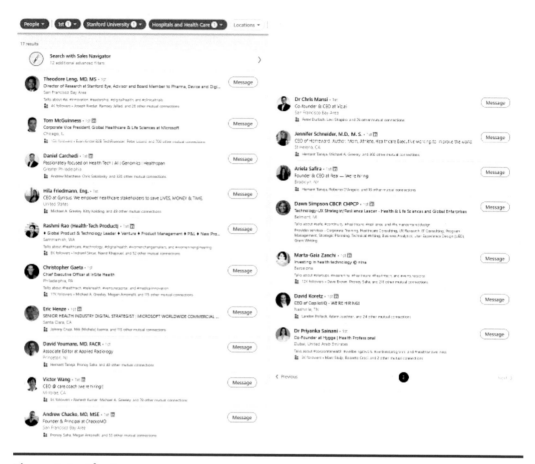

Figure 6.3   The team.

Source: © Sally Ann Frank

route. In Figure 6.4, I show where you can post your jobs as well as some samples from the team at Hyro.

But perhaps the best strategy for hiring is to ask industry peers, colleagues, and trusted allies who understand what you are trying to accomplish and the type of talent you need. While a friend may not be the best choice, a friend of a friend might be perfect.

It's also important to note, especially in the early stages, that not everyone has to be a full-time employee, especially subject matter experts who are not needed on a daily basis, like your attorney, CFO, and regulatory specialist. Or they can be more operational types, like a fractional marketer, alliance manager, or administrative assistant who you need for specific projects or to fill in gaps until you can hire. You can contract with organizations that place fractional experts with your startup. In a Forbes article, written by Sergui Matei on fractional hiring, he comments that,

Figure 6.4   Job posts on LinkedIn.

Source: LinkedIn Portal

Fractional hiring is today what freelance work was 20 years ago. It reflects the current zeitgeist around work culture and could be just the thing to alleviate cash flow issues while also providing a mutually beneficial relationship between you and new employees.[4]

In this same Forbes article, he shares some of the risks of fractional hires and how to avoid them, including setting clear expectations, treating fractional employees the same as full-time employees (just with fewer hours and less pay), ensuring there is a non-compete clause in the contract, and maintaining consistent and clear communications.

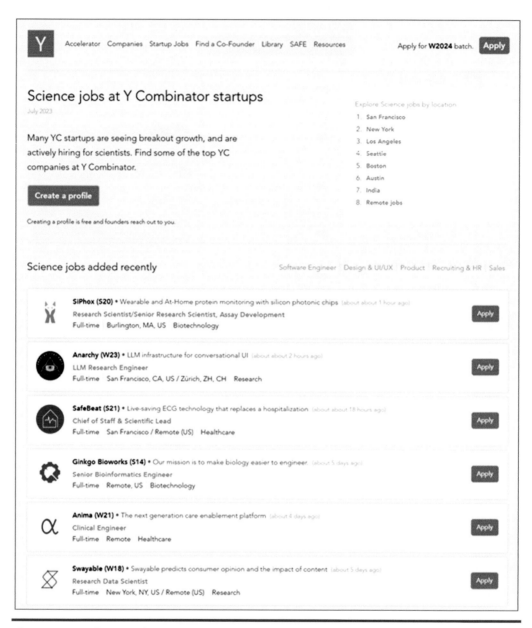

Figure 6.5 Job posts from accelerators.

Source: Science jobs at Y Combinator startups | Y Combinator https://www.ycombinator.com/jobs/role/science

Another option for finding the right team is to work with the accelerator program in which you are participating. Some accelerators, like Y Combinator, post job openings from startups on their website (Figure 6.5), which can be immensely helpful, especially if you are looking for colleagues who have previously worked in startups. (More on accelerators in Chapter 8.)

The Tribe

If your team are your employees, both full-time and fractional, your tribe are your advisors, cheerleaders, and influencers who want to see you succeed and will do what they can to support you. These people are willing to use their network to your benefit, boost your social media posts, offer guidance when asked (and sometimes when it's not), and basically go out of their way to help you build your business.

Again, LinkedIn is a terrific way to build your tribe, by inviting all your relevant contacts to follow your company page and producing newsletters that you can push to your contacts as well. In addition to this digital engagement, finding champions that you can meet in person is even more helpful.

The best way to build your tribe (and possibly your pipeline) is to go where your tribe is already located. Through industry events, like HIMSS and HLTH (which both offer events outside the United States), not only can you meet with prospective customers, but you can also build your tribe. Additionally, many regions have their own communities and events for healthcare and life sciences innovators. Lastly, find events where you can speak and share your passion for the problem you are solving.

Which brings me to an especially important point – who is your chief evangelist? Without someone who can tell your story with passion, commitment, and empathy, you may never get out of the metaphorical stage of two people working in a garage. Those of us in digital health know both the value and the perils of charisma when building a company, all too well. Elizabeth Holmes was the queen when it came to passion, charisma, and salesmanship. But charisma without a solution is doomed as well.

When I think of charismatic entrepreneurs who quickly and easily add to their tribe, I think of my own experience with founders. One of the founders who rises to the top in this area is Ellington West of Sonavi Labs. Just by hearing the Sonavi Labs story with passion, excitement, and impact, listeners are enamored with their mission, the device, and how they plan to revolutionize the diagnosis and treatment of respiratory diseases. (If you want to see Ellington in action, check out this video taken at SXSW where they were the Health, Wearables & Wellbeing Winner in 2022, https://youtu.be/xDm_kT1vFes.)

When building your tribe, consider going after influencers in your area of specialization. Begin by following them on LinkedIn and any other channels they may be using and see what they post and what interests them. From there, you can begin to engage with them, connect with them, and build rapport, which could lead to a meeting or a joint podcast or something that will propel your company and solution to a larger audience.

For example, I followed Joseph Kvedar (https://www.linkedin.com/in /joekvedar/) on LinkedIn and Twitter after reading his books, *The New Mobile Age* (https://joekvedar.com/books/the-new-mobile-age/) and *The Internet of Healthy Things* (https://theinternetofhealthythings.com/). I saw him speak at numerous industry events on telehealth and virtual healthcare, and after some time, I got the courage to message him through LinkedIn. A few weeks later I found myself having coffee at an industry with Dr Kvedar (and I had him sign my copy of his book!). I was practically giddy to be able to meet a thought leader like Dr Kvedar in person. You can and should do the same for people who can not only help you in elevating your status in the ecosystem but can become a trusted advisor and advocate.

The Corporate Identity

Now that you have your team and tribe, what is the rallying cry? Who are you and what do you stand for? For many people, when they think of launching a company, coming up with a name, logo, mission statement, etc. is creative and exciting. For others, it's a slog and the sooner it's over the better. Regardless of where you sit on that continuum, there are some basic rules that you can apply to your company brand.

The Company Name

Please, please, please, make it a pronounceable name. Don't just string letters together. Let your company name have meaning that is easily conveyed to your customers, partners, and stakeholders. One of my favorite healthcare startup names is Fabric Health (https://www.fabrichealth.org/), a company dedicated to offering healthcare services to underserved communities by setting up clinics in laundromats. The name, Fabric Health, is inextricably linked to its mission, while intimating what they do in just two words. Another favorite is BehaVR, (https://www.behavr.com/). Pronounced "behavior" they offer solutions to improve mental health using virtual reality. Now you get it, right? Another good one is Recuro Health (https://recurohealth .com/) which offers virtual primary care and several other healthcare services, through their Digital Medical Home™. Their name Recuro is Latin for cure, restore, or refresh, making it a great name for this telehealth company. This article from Entrepreneur magazine is a good primer with practical advice on naming a company.

Also remember that while your logo and mission may (and probably will) evolve, it is likely that your company name is forever. Pick wisely, carefully, and thoughtfully. If you plan to operate globally, also confirm that your chosen name translates well in other languages.

The Logo

I'm not a graphic artist, but we have all seen logos that resonate with the brand and instill a sense of affinity, and those that don't. Surprisingly, Microsoft Create has an interesting take on the importance of a good logo:

> A logo is a visual symbol representing your brand. It's not your entire brand, but it is an important piece. Your brand is made up of other various elements that create a whole visual and messaging system. However, the logo can often be the first visual interaction someone has with your brand. Just like a first impression, a logo isn't everything, but it is important.[5]

Additionally, with the advent of DALL-E, you can experiment on your own with Bing.com. For example, I put in this prompt, "generate a logo that is simple and sophisticated for a digital health company with hands" and I got what you see here in Figure 6.6:

Figure 6.6   The logos from DALL-E.

Source: Bing.com

Now clearly, some of these are pretty goofy, but the bottom left one isn't too bad. And you can see where this might be the starting point for you to conceptualize your logo and then take it to an actual human being to refine. There are plenty of virtual services out there that do this, like fiverr.com and 99Designs, or you may prefer to work with someone you already know. Regardless, remember that your logo is likely to evolve with the company, leaving you room for future refinement.

A few of my favorite startup logos are included in Figure 6.7.

Figure 6.7   Cool startup logos.

Source: Pangaea Data, Active Surgical, Faro Health, Heart-Tech Health and Fabric Health. Permission to print these logos has been granted to the author.

The Mission Statement

Your mission statement may also evolve, but it's important to articulate it in easy-to-understand language that will appeal to your target customers, partners, and stakeholders. It also must be appealing for prospective employees. No one wants to go to work for a company that, "processes medical images to detect abnormalities." Instead, they want to work for a company that, "uses AI to identify potential breast cancer earlier than traditional mammography" (I'm making this up, of course, but you get the point).

What is your mission? One of my favorites is from Pangaea Data. They use their mission statement in everything they do because it's clear, concise and goes something like this (I'm paraphrasing):

Pangaea Data uses AI to characterize patients who were previously underdiagnosed, misdiagnosed, or miscoded, so they can get the care they need and participate in relevant clinical trials and therapies.

You understand what they do, right? And while this isn't a value proposition, it does start to reveal the benefits and value for providers, pharmaceutical companies, and patients. In one sentence, they have covered it all. This mission statement is so easy to understand and tangible, that shortly after meeting them, I was able to recite it almost verbatim. Their website home page reiterates this brand statement, and you can check it out at https://www .pangaeadata.ai/.

When building your mission statement, it's imperative that you refrain from jargon and acronyms and be as clear as possible. Let's look at another mission statement, this time from MedCrypt, a cybersecurity company focused on securing medical devices. Their mission statement is:

MedCrypt provides data security as a service to medical device OEMs. From medical imaging device[s] to implantable devices like pacemakers, MedCrypt ensures that devices act only on instructions from trusted sources.[6]

This one is a bit more technical and they could do a better job on the "trusted sources" part, but if you are a medical equipment manufacturer (OEM), you get it and understand their mission right away.

With the advent of ChatGPT, you can get AI to help you craft your mission statement. Copy.ai has a template you can check out at https://www .copy.ai/templates/company-mission-statement?via=NPM. And just for fun, I asked Bing.com to help me with a mission statement for a telehealth company that specializes in serving rural communities and this is what I got in one attempt:

Our mission is to provide quality healthcare services to rural communities in the US through telehealth. We aim to increase access to physicians, specialists, and other healthcare services for patients in rural, frontier, and underserved areas. Our goal is to reduce or minimize challenges and burdens patients encounter, such as transportation issues related to traveling for specialty care. We strive to improve monitoring, timeliness, and communications within the healthcare system.

Source: Conversation with Bing, 6/29/2023. These are the sites that Bing Chat used to come up with the mission statement:

(1) Telehealth Use in Rural Healthcare – Rural Health Information Hub. https://www.ruralhealthinfo.org/topics/telehealth.

(2) I. Introduction – Rural Health. https://www.ruralhealth.us/ NRHA/media/Emerge_NRHA/Advocacy/Policy%20documents /2019-NRHA-Policy-Document-Telehealth-In-Rural-America.pdf.

(3) Office for the Advancement of Telehealth | HRSA – Health Resources and … https://www.hrsa.gov/rural-health/topics/telehealth.

(4) Our Vision, Mission and Values | Access TeleCare. https:// accesstelecare.com/our-vision-mission-and-values/.

(5) Introduction to Rural Telehealth | Telehealth.HHS.gov. https:// telehealth.hhs.gov/providers/best-practice-guides/telehealth-for -rural-areas.

Not too bad – again, just like the image for a logo – it needs some refinement, but it is better than looking at a blank screen!

The Value Proposition

The value proposition takes your mission one step further and articulates the quantitative results customers can expect from your solution. Investopedia defines a value proposition as:

> A value proposition stands as a promise by a company to a customer or market segment. The proposition is an easy-to-understand reason why a customer should buy a product or service from that particular business. A value proposition should clearly explain how a product fills a need, communicate the specifics of its added benefit, and state the reason why it's better than similar products on the market. The ideal value proposition is to-the-point and appeals to a customer's strongest decision-making drivers.[7]

In my experience, many founders forget this part altogether. They will go into great detail about what their solution does and why, but neglect to include the tangible benefits customers will receive. You can include quantitative and qualitative benefits in your value proposition. Figure 6.8 highlights a few examples of benefits in healthcare and life sciences.

Quantitative Benefits	Qualitative Benefits
• Reducing the cost of care • Reducing labor costs • Adding new revenue streams	• Reducing staff and clinician burnout • Reducing patient readmissions • Improving patient outcomes

Figure 6.8 Sample benefits.

Source: © Sally Ann Frank

Every value proposition should include quantitative results, when possible, although when you are first starting out, this is literally impossible if you have no customers. However, in healthcare and life sciences, we do a LOT of testing, in some cases, before the business even exists. In those cases, where the early indicators prove the solution is effective (why else would you be building a company around it), using those quantitative results is an option. Subsequently, the moment you have a customer, even if in a validation or trial stage, you should begin gathering quantitative data to make your value proposition more meaningful.

You can also look at your value proposition as a formula, like this:[8]

[Product or service] helps [target customer] [benefit] by [differentiation].

The approach appeals to me because it clearly includes all the key elements. They go on to provide some examples:

[Spotify] can assist [music lovers] in [discovering and enjoying millions of songs] with [personalized playlists and unlimited streaming].
[Grammarly] can aid [writers] in [improving their writing] through [checking and correcting grammar, spelling, and tone].[9]

I'm not a huge fan of these, but you get the idea. I would opt for including more quantitative details. For example, this one for our fictional telehealth company focused on rural and underserved communities:

[Frank Health] helps [patients in rural areas] [meet with clinicians within 30 minutes, without having to travel for hours] using our [always-on, virtual network of providers].

Or going a bit more high-tech, check out this one for a fictitious AI-infused imaging solution:

> [Frank Imaging Solutions] helps [clinician] [diagnose pneumonia in seconds] using [AI-powered algorithms that integrate easily into workflows and accelerate treatment].

Your value proposition will likely evolve over time, so be open to subtle changes in how you state it. Once written, be sure to test it out with your proxy customers to make sure they understand and can relate to it.

The Tagline

The tagline is your abbreviated value proposition. Merriam-Webster says a tagline can also be a slogan:

> a reiterated phrase identified with an individual, group, or product: SLOGAN.[10]

It may also be part of your logo or appear with your logo on your website and other marketing assets. Your tagline will and should evolve over time, and may be something you wait to develop, especially if a tagline doesn't seem needed immediately. Think about your own experiences. There may be taglines that you remember because they were catchy, evoked a strong image, or embodied the brand strongly. As you begin to think about a possible tagline, remember those taglines you thought were effective as examples. Here are a few digital health taglines that I think work well:

- **Faro Health** – Together, we can improve lives by simplifying clinical research
- **Infinadeck** – The movement platform for the metaverse
- **Activ Surgical** – Seeing beyond the visible
- **Pangaea Data** – Characterizing patients, mapping patient journey & disease trajectories

The Website

A website is the digital embodiment of your company. It will include your logo, value proposition, mission statement, and tagline. Think of it as the front door to your company from anywhere in the world. It too, will evolve over time. As your company matures, so will your website. Below is a quick map of what your website should include at each stage. Note that the website attributes are additive; as you grow your website will include more information and options to interact with you.

Startup stage	Website attributes	Function
Ideate	• Single page • Company name • Contact info • Social channels • Anything else you want to share	Secure URL Post "coming soon"
Build	• Multiple pages • Problem you are solving • How you are solving it • Founding team & advisors • Job openings • CTA: Join us or follow us on social channels	Generate interest Attract employees, advisors, tribe members
Launch	• Details on research, validation or other projects • News and media mentions • CTA: Contact us to be a test or validation site	Attract early adopters Begin posting promotional materials
Grow	• Blogs • Customer stories • White papers, videos, podcasts, etc. • CTA: Contact us for a demo, download a white paper, meet us at HIMSS (or some other industry event)	Sell your solution Attract customers, distribution & channel partners

Figure 6.9 **Website development stages.**

Source: © Sally Ann Frank

The Business Model

"How do you make money?" This is a question I have repeated more times than I'd like to admit when talking to founders. Unfortunately, the responses are not always clear. Healthcare and life sciences founders are different from typical startup founders. Often, HLS founders are more mission- than profit-driven because they are clinicians, academicians, or others who have had a profound health event themselves or within their close circle of families and friends. That's admirable and frankly, I love to see that passion. But making money while you save the world enables you to continue to save the world in new ways.

In this SaaS world, your business model is going to be based on consumption. Just how that consumption is measured is up to you. Here are some examples using our fictitious AI-powered imaging company:

- **By transaction** – How many images will the algorithm scan?
- **By user** – How many users will use the algorithm?
- **By site** – How many locations will use the algorithm?

It's important to note that these are not mutually exclusive. In fact, many companies offer all three of these options to respond to various market segments. Additionally, some SaaS companies offer a freemium version of their solution as a gateway to paying subscriptions. Some of the best-known brands globally offer freemium versions, including Spotify, which was mentioned above.

Continuing with our AI-power algorithm example, you might find a business model like the one presented in Figure 6.10:

Business model	Pricing
Freemium	$0 with a max of 5 scans per month
By transaction	$10 per image scanned
By user	$150 per user per month
By site	$5,000 per site up to 10,000 scans
	$10,000 per site up to 25,000 scans
	$30,000 per site up to 60,000 scans
	$50,000 per site for unlimited scans

Figure 6.10   The business model.

Source: © Sally Ann Frank

Again, this is just an example, following a pattern that has been proven and followed by global brands to small startups. What is most important is to build this model *based on your costs*. Go back to your investor deck and the historical P&L and burn rate spreadsheet and then build your pricing model based on what you need to be profitable over time. Then do your best to check out competitors or adjacent solutions and see how they price their solution.

If you've never built a business model before, you may want to check out The York Group (https://theyorkgroup.com/), an organization dedicated to helping companies sort out the intricacies of building a SaaS business. Additionally, they have some excellent resources on their website, including a few ebooks and

an extensive library of short-form videos (2–8 minutes) that cover most of the questions companies have when it comes to developing the right Cloud business strategy. Topics include market selection, pricing, sales organization & sales compensation, how to build and support productive channels, customer support, legal issues and more.[11]

They even have special offers for Microsoft partners (https://theyorkgroup .com/microsoft-partners/). Additionally, you may want to follow their CEO, Harald Horgan, on LinkedIn (https://www.linkedin.com/in/hhorgen/) to get a better understanding of what The York Group does and what is important to them in the world of SaaS business development.

Besides your pricing model, your business model also needs to include key elements like deployment services, customer support, software updates, security updates, and other items that you may not have considered yet. Depending on your plans, you can choose to outsource these services, partner with a larger organization, or with the right level of funding, hire experts to address these areas. Here are some things to consider:

- **Deployment services** – Even in a SaaS world, someone must install software and possibly integrate the solution into an existing system (like an electronic medical record system) or workflow. Is this something you plan to do? Will you have to build a software development kit (SDK) or application programming interface (API) to streamline this process?
- **Customer support** – Will you have your own customer support team, or will you outsource this function? Will they be available 24/7? How will you train them, keep them trained, and enable them to keep your customers happy? How will their experiences inform your product development road map? How will you support your first few customers, before you are generating revenue?
- **Software updates** – How will these be done over the air (OTA) safely and securely? How do you keep track of which customers have which version of your software? Will you charge for updates that improve functionality or accuracy? How will you comply with the FDA's Predetermined Change Control Plan for Artificial Intelligence/Machine Learning (AI/ML)- Enabled Device Software Functions,[12] if this applies to your solution?
- **Security updates** – How will you manage security updates when the threats to healthcare and life sciences companies continue to explode? (The healthcare sector suffered about 295 breaches in the first half of 2023 alone, according to the HHS Office for Civil Rights (OCR) data breach portal. More than 39 million individuals were implicated in healthcare data breaches in the first 6 months of the year.[13])

When finalizing your business model, you may need to consider how value-based care figures into your pricing approach. According to the New England Journal of Medicine:

> Value-based healthcare is a healthcare delivery model in which providers, including hospitals and physicians, are paid based on patient health outcomes. Under value-based care agreements, providers are rewarded for helping patients improve their health, reduce the effects and incidence of chronic disease, and live healthier lives in an evidence-based way.
>
> Value-based care differs from a fee-for-service or capitated approach, in which providers are paid based on the amount of healthcare services they deliver. The "value" in value-based healthcare is derived from measuring health outcomes against the cost of delivering the outcomes.[14]

How your provider customers get paid could affect your business model. There's no right or wrong answer here; just be aware of their business model and make sure that yours doesn't introduce unneeded complexity.

The Regulatory Journey

Chapter 3 details many of the regulations that you need to consider in the United States and select regions around the world. Unless you have prior experience with regulatory compliance, it's most likely you will have to find, hire, or retain a regulatory expert. This is definitely not an area in which you can skimp. Consider calling up one of the legal firms listed in Chapter 3 or working with an organization like HITRUST Alliance (https://hitrust-alliance.net/) or Drata (https://drata.com/) that can help you and provide automated tools to maintain compliant at all times.

From the perspective of building your company, your regulatory journey must be well-planned and tightly coupled with your product development and go-to-market strategies. Ideally, the three parts of your business should be documented and mapped out with timelines, the critical path, and interdependencies. Unfortunately, I don't have an example to share, as these types of tools are highly confidential and not shareable. Instead, I put together a simple chart in Figure 6.11 to show what this might look like in your startup, using our fictitious company, Frank Imaging Solutions.

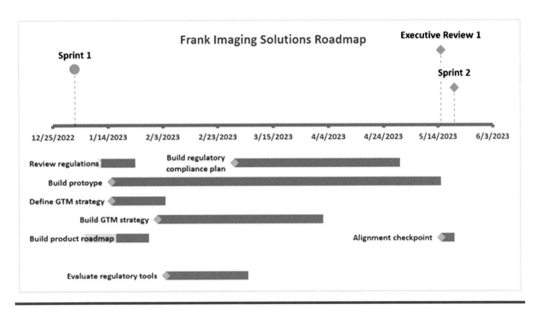

Figure 6.11   The regulatory journey.

Source: © Sally Ann Frank

The Allure of Stealth

As you begin to build your company, there is a lot of excitement, angst, and uncertainty. For many, this means going into "stealth mode," essentially operating in secret to protect your intellectual property (IP). This feels like a safer thing to do. However, if just talking about your company is a risk that enables others to build something similar, then you should just stop. To me (and most investors), a company that is in stealth mode is not viable in the long-term due to a lack of competitive advantage.

On the other hand, if you channel those feelings of excitement, angst, and uncertainty into positive energy, you will probably find people are willing and even eager to support you, make meaningful connections for you, and help you find resources and team members. Resist the urge to go stealth and if you feel you must, go back and review your solution and your company. Evaluate if there really is a barrier to entry for potential competitors. If there isn't a significant barrier, can you change something about your company or solution that does raise the bar? If not, you probably need to come up with another idea for your startup.

Summary

Pitfall	Best Practice
Assuming you will be wildly successful	Consider the key elements of your company • What is your value proposition? • How will you align product development, regulatory and GTM workstreams? • Does your company and solution have competitive advantage?

Resources

- The Viability of the Digital Healthcare Sector in 2023 (forbes.com).
- How to Create a Successful Value Proposition (forbes.com).
- How to Write a Great Value Proposition [7 Top Examples + Template] (hubspot.com).
- The Rise of the Contract Executive theworkplacereport.cmail20.com/t/d-e-vztrtd-irjuwdjhd-r/.
- How to Name a Business: 7 Helpful Tips | Entrepreneur(https://www.entrepreneur.com/starting-a-business/7-tips-for-naming-your-business/223401).
- How to Design a Logo for Your Brand or Business | Learn at Microsoft Create (https://create.microsoft.com/en-us/learn/articles/how-to-design-brand-business-logo).
- The 30 Best and Most Famous Brand Slogans and Taglines (https://www.adobe.com/express/learn/blog/30-companies-with-famous-brand-slogans-taglines).

Notes

1. More Evidence That Company Diversity Leads to Better Profits (forbes.com).
2. Things to Consider When Hiring Family Members (forbes.com).
3. Ellington West Is on Inc.'s 2021 Female Founders 100 list.
4. Fractional Hiring Can Make a Lot of Sense for Startups—Here's How To Do It (forbes.com).
5. How to Design a Logo for Your Brand or Business | Learn at Microsoft Create.
6. MedCrypt: Overview | LinkedIn.
7. Value Proposition: How to Write It with Examples (investopedia.com).

8. How to Write a Value Proposition Statement That Sells (https://www.linkedin .com/advice/0/what-key-elements-value-proposition-statement-how.

9. How to Write a Value Proposition Statement That Sells (linkedin.com).

10. Tagline Definition & Meaning – Merriam-Webster.

11. Resources – The York Group.

12. https://www.fda.gov/regulatory-information/search-fda-guidance-documents/ marketing-submission-recommendations-predetermined-change-control-plan -artificial.

13. Biggest Healthcare Data Breaches Reported This Year, So Far (healthitsecurity .com).

14. What Is Value-Based Healthcare? | NEJM Catalyst.

Chapter 7

The Pitch

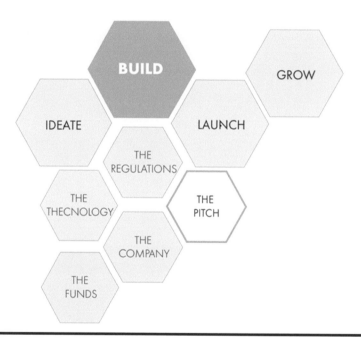

Figure 7.1   The pitch.

Source: © Sally Ann Frank

> *Everyone understands the value of what we are doing and will buy it.*

It can be painful to watch startup pitches. I'll share one recent experience that was excruciating to watch. I was at a medical conference in California where we had set up a special session so practitioners could hear about cool new technologies coming their way. Most of the presenting startups had achieved product-market fit, so (theoretically) their pitches should have

DOI: 10.4324/9781032639468-7

been well-honed. With ten startups on the docket, the pitches were going well. Everyone was adhering to the five-minute limit for their pitches and responded well to the five-minute Q&A that followed. Until about half way through the program, when a clinician-founder took the podium.

It's hard to know where to start, but it was a disastrous pitch that failed in so many ways. Now, there are plenty of clinician-founders who know how to pitch, so this is not to imply that clinician-founders are not good presenters. It's just this one that wasn't, and frankly, the mistakes she made are common ones.

First, she spent far too much time talking about herself and not enough time talking about the company, the problem she was trying to solve, and her solution. Second, she meandered around a variety of topics that seemed very random. Third, she did not end at the five-minute mark, and when asked to finish (several times), she rambled on for ten more minutes. Fourth, by the time her 15-minute pitch was over, the audience had little idea about her value proposition. Fifth, there was no call to action to contact her for additional information, or request a demo, or any number of things to generate a sales opportunity.

To be successful, you need to be able to pitch clearly, consistently, and concisely. You also need to adjust your mindset. Instead of thinking and speaking in terms of, "we do this," say, "we can do this for you." Be humble and helpful, not aggressive and arrogant.

We have already covered the investor pitch deck; now, we will address the sales pitch deck, which is similar but not the same.

Personas

But before digging into content, let's talk about your audience for these pitches. You may find yourself in a pitch competition at some event or accelerator, which is great. Never turn down an opportunity to pitch, as it's always good to practice and you learn from the responses you receive.

However, in this section, we are specifically addressing the people you expect to see in a traditional sales call. There are a couple of ways to break down the personas you are going to meet: (1) by their title; and (2) role in the buying process.

Titles

In healthcare, we typically think about clinicians and business leaders as buyers. But you also must think about technology leaders, security leaders, and administrative leaders, just to name a few. Map out your personas by title and alter your pitch based on who is in the room, virtual or otherwise. Typical persona titles may include these titles or directors and managers that report to these executives:

- Chief medical officer (CMO)
- Chief medical information officer (CMIO)
- Chief nursing information officer (CNIO)
- Chief medical affairs officer
- Chief digital officer (CDO)
- Chief information officer (CIO)
- Chief technical officer (CTO)
- Chief revenue cycle officer
- Chief information security officer (CISO)
- Chief administrative officer (CAO)
- Chief strategy officer
- Chief patient engagement officer
- Chief Innovation officer

Roles

Roles are particularly important and different from titles when mapping out personas. Ideally, you want to match a title with a buying process role to really understand who you are working with and what is important to them. There are many different models for the roles that participate in the buying process, but this list in Figure 7.2 compiles the things I have learned and believe to be most relevant

It's important to note that these personas are not finite or mutually exclusive. You can have a champion who is a business decision maker, or a detractor who is a technical decision maker. Be cognizant of who you are working with, how they view you and your solution, and the connections they can broker or block.

The Buying Process

Every customer buys differently, but it's important to be aware of the process at a macro level to make sure you include the right people at the right time. You will want to have these people involved most likely in this order:

Role	Characteristics	How to work with them
Detractors	Will do what they can to prevent a purchase of your solution	Be as friendly as possible, knowing that they are not going to help you; don't share any confidential business information that they could use to inform the competition
"Seemores"	Easily builds rapport, always asking for more information but typically has no buying power or authority	Do the minimum to keep this person happy, lest they move to detractor role
Influencers	Can help you win the deal, but require a more senior person to purchase the solution	Work closely with influencers until you reach the executive buyer, and then bring them along on that journey, working to make your influencer look good to the higher ups
Business decision makers	Typically, are evaluating the economics of your solution and trying to figure out the ROI, impact to operations, and burden of adopting a new solution	Use qualitative and quantitative value statements that will make your solution attractive
Technical decision makers	Usually are evaluating the technical aspects of your solution, how it will integrate with existing systems, how you will support it, and how hard it will be to get users to use it	Use the same qualitative and quantitative approach but in terms of how your solution will positively affect the IT department and technical restructure; do your best to show how your solution will make their lives easier
Champions	Your best advocate, but may not have the decision-making authority to buy	Keep these people close and have them help you navigate through the organization to orchestrate your deal
Gate Keepers	They direct access (or erect obstacles) between you and many of the folks above	Often more administrative in nature, being easy to work with, respectful and gracious is the best way to win these people over and gain access to the decision makers

Figure 7.2   Buying roles.

Source: © Sally Ann Frank

1. **Clinical champion** – This person can be the CMO, CMIO, CNIO, or someone in charge of a service line, like cardiology. In pharma, this person might be a scientist, clinician, business unit leader, or medical affairs leader.
2. **Security leader** – This person is likely to be the CISO but may also be a CIO or CTO. They will be charged with ensuring your solution meets the organization's security and privacy requirements. Furthermore, they will want to make sure that your solution doesn't increase their risk of cyberattacks.
3. **CIO/CTO** – Charged with interoperability, integration, and maintaining IT standards, they will be focused on how easy it is to implement and support your solution. The easier you make it for them (i.e., turn-key, or

plug-and-play) the more likely they are to vote yes about buying your solution.

4. **Procurement** – Once the purchase decision is to be made, these are the people you will be negotiating final terms with. This is also where the marketplaces of Microsoft and other vendors may speed up the process.

You may have noticed that I didn't specifically identify innovation leaders in this list. That is due to the varying nature of their influence in the buying process. Some innovation teams are driven by business needs, focused on applied innovation, and part of the buying process. Other innovation teams are charged with understanding trends and testing new technologies in more of a lab setting but are not part of the procurement process. Be sure to (gently) ask the role of any innovative leader or team that you encounter to understand their ability to influence buying decisions.

Keep in mind that most buying decisions are made by a committee. This becomes especially important when you are discussing a free trial or proof of concept. You may find yourself working with someone, investing time, effort, and energy, only to find that person is an outlier and has little (or possibly no) standing with the members of the buying committee.

Lastly, you will want to understand the financial health, budgeting cycles, strategic plans, key executives, and other key characteristics of your target customers. For public companies, this will be a straightforward search on the web. For private organizations, you may have to get more creative, relying on your champion or influencer to share these types of details. Moreover, safety net hospitals and academic medical centers typically purchase solutions in ways that may vary dramatically from for-profit hospitals and pharmaceutical, life sciences, and medical device companies. The sooner you can understand the buying process of your customers, the more accurately you will be able to direct your limited sales efforts toward opportunities with a higher probability of closing.

The Deck

Now that you know who you are going to meet and how they may react, it's time to create your pitch deck. This pitch deck is specifically for prospects and differs slightly from your investor pitch deck. Figure 7.3 shows how the

Topic	Investor	Customer
Title page	√	√
The ask	√	
The problem	√	√
The value proposition	√	√
The management team	√	√
The competitive advantage	√	√
The competitive analysis	√	
Business model	√	
GTM plan	√	
Financials	√	
Progress to date	√	√
Current customers		√
Offer		√
Call to action		√
Total number of slides	**11**	**9**

Figure 7.3   The investor and customer decks.

Source: © Sally Ann Frank

content differs between investor decks and pitch decks, so you can easily see which slides you can reuse.

The remainder of this section will focus on the slides that are unique to the customer pitch deck, namely, Current Customers, Offer, and Call to Action. But before we do that, let's review the problem slide. As mentioned in Chapter 3, we noted that AEYE Health quickly conveys the problem they are solving with high impact graphics. If you are struggling with how to position the problem that you are solving, consider starting with:

> What if you could [solve problem] by [taking action that your solution offers] to [value]?

For our faux Frank Imaging Solutions, that problem statement could be:

> What if you could [quickly diagnose pneumonia] by [using AI] to [speed treatment to patients]?

Play around with that syntax and see if it helps you clarify the problem you are trying to solve.

The Current Customers

In this section of your customer pitch deck, you include any organizations that are working with you, whether they are paying you or not. In healthcare and life sciences, we do a LOT of validation, often without pay, drawing on the funds from angel investors, or from a pre-seed round of funding. If you are accurate and have the approval of your customers, share what you are doing and with whom. If your customers are not willing to be named, then describe the type of company in your customer slide. Instead of putting a logo from your top pharma customer, you could simply say, "a large multi-national pharmaceutical company." But be certain that you don't give away details that the customer doesn't want divulged. Also note that some customers will do personal references even if they are not comfortable having their logo on your slide. Be ready with that reference in your back pocket, if needed.

I put this slide together as an example shown in Figure 7.4, but ideally it would include the logos from the customers who have given you express permission (that you document and keep) to share your work with them.

The Offer

The offer should tell your prospects how they can purchase your product. This goes back to our business model discussion, and the offer should be a manifestation of your business model. A successful founder will always present an offer, even it if wasn't requested. (For those who are or were salespeople, it's the old assumptive close, "Would you like to buy the blue or red car?") Less successful founders will go through their entire customer pitch without giving the prospect a way to move forward. Nothing is more

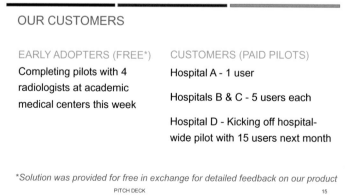

OUR CUSTOMERS

EARLY ADOPTERS (FREE*)

Completing pilots with 4 radiologists at academic medical centers this week

CUSTOMERS (PAID PILOTS)

Hospital A - 1 user

Hospitals B & C - 5 users each

Hospital D - Kicking off hospital-wide pilot with 15 users next month

*Solution was provided for free in exchange for detailed feedback on our product

PITCH DECK   15

Figure 7.4   Current customers.

Source: © Sally Ann Frank

deflating than watching a great pitch, seeing the customer get excited, and then have the founder end with, "Well, that's my pitch."

You may be thinking, "But how do I even know if they want to buy my product?" You don't, and that's ok. By extending the offer, you get valuable experience:

1. **Seeing how prospects respond** – to the price, structure, and other elements of your offer
2. **Getting feedback on your solution** – to understand how you compare with competitors and how well you are responding to market trends
3. **Practicing asking for the deal** – to ensure that you are comfortable with the messaging and economics of your offer

It's important not to confuse the offer with the call to action. The offer is how the customer can buy. The call to action is the customer's next step in their journey with you. Keep in mind that if you are early in your journey, and don't have an offer yet, you can still engage them with a call to action. Below is an example of an offer. In fact, as you will see in Figure 7.5, integrate.AI presents multiple offers that their prospects can choose from. Ideally, this would also include pricing for your different offers.

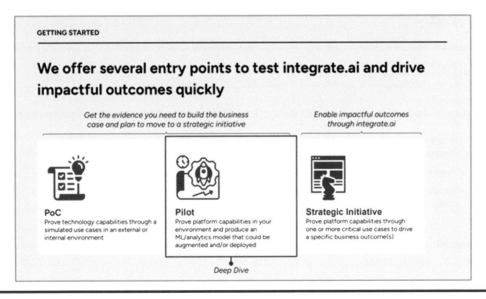

Figure 7.5   The offer.

Source: Pitch deck – next steps – Integrate.ai, Steve Irvine

The Call to Action

There are two types of calls to action; one is related to your offer and the other is in lieu of an offer. Let's start with the one that is related to your offer.

You have just pitched our imaginary AI algorithm for diagnosing pneumonia. You have outlined the various pricing models, and everyone is still in the room or on the video call. Great! Now what? You present your call to action. In this case, where you have a product you can sell, your call to action could be:

- Demonstrating the solution
- Meeting to discuss the buying process and a pilot project
- Organizing a call with a reference customer
- Sharing relevant clinical data and research

The goal of the call to action is to move forward in the sales process, by *adding value for all involved.* I have seen plenty of situations where follow on meetings are merely repeats with a slightly different set of attendees. If you have a prospective client who is continuing to ask for more information without helping you close the deal, you have just met a Seemore (and you should disengage). Figure 7.6 is an example that shows some potential calls to action that add value for the prospect and you.

NEXT STEPS

See a demonstration	Review clinical data	Check tech infrastructure
• Participate in 30-minute meeting • See a brief demo • Discuss workflow integration	• Share clinical studies • Review and answer any questions • Discuss relevance to your patient population	• Discuss integrating solution with existing tech infrastructure • Develop a rough implementation timeline • Conduct a security audit, when appropriate

Figure 7.6 **Next steps.**

Source: © Sally Ann Frank

Remember to customize your pitch deck for your audience. How you discuss your solution should be different when talking to a chief medical officer versus a chief technical officer. For the CMO, you may need to add a slide about your clinical validation; while for the CTO, you may need to add a slide about your technical architecture and how the patient data is secured.

The Caveats

There are a few mistakes that I see repeatedly that I'd like to share, to help you improve your pitch to a prospect.

- **Do your homework** – Take 30 minutes well-ahead of the meeting to review the prospect's website and figure out how your solution fits in with their strategy. Look at recent annual reports, articles, and press releases. Search LinkedIn for the people you are meeting and look at their backgrounds. See what they post and learn what's important to them. Identify common contacts who may come in handy later. You may even find common interests on which you can quickly build rapport.
- **Presentation order** – Start with the problem you are solving and how. Don't start with the company history or your background. If they don't like your solution, the backstory becomes irrelevant. I would recommend the order shown in Figure 7.7.
- **Business value** – Don't rely on customers to derive your business value for themselves. If you don't state it, most of them will miss it. Too

Slide	Topic
Title page	Include your contact information, social channels
The problem	Outline why you want to solve it
The value proposition	Describe how you are solving the problem and the benefits to your customer
The management team	Convey why this team can solve this problem
The competitive advantage	Highlight what makes you different
Progress to date	Showcase what you have accomplished regarding trials, regulatory compliance, etc.
Current customers	Share paying or not paying depending on the stage of your company, remembering to keep customers' names private if asked to do so
Offer	Detail how the customer can buy your solution
Next steps (call to action)	Recommend the next steps in the buying journey

Figure 7.7   Presentation order.

Source: © Sally Ann Frank

often, I have heard a startup founder or representative end with, "So, that's what we do. What do you think?" Be overt with your business value through your value proposition. Be clear, concise, and consistent in describing how your solution will help the customer. Tell them how your solution will benefit them specifically, based on the research you did prior to the meeting.

- **Read the room** – This is a bit trickier when presenting virtually. Regardless of whether you are pitching in person or over a webcam, include pauses and questions to your audience at key points in your presentation. Your script may look something like the outline in Figure 7.8.

  - In-person – If you are presenting to an in-person group, watch them. Are they checking their phones and checking out? Or are they leaning in (literally) and actively listening? If the audience seems disengaged, stop the presentation. Really. Ask if what you are presenting isn't what they expected. Ask for feedback on what you've presented so far and engage them in conversation to see if there is a disconnect or if you need to customize your presentation a bit more.

  - Virtually – If you are presenting virtually, suggest (gently) that everyone be on camera. Typically, off camera folks are not paying as close attention as those on camera. Start your pitch by asking, "Can everyone see my deck? And you can hear and see me as well?" From there, watch or have a colleague watch for virtual hand raises and comments in the meeting chat. Unless a question is irrelevant, always pause to answer a question or respond to a comment – even if you are mid-sentence. Even more so in a virtual setting,

Topic
Title page
The problem
PAUSE: Ask if this is a problem within their organization and how they are dealing with it today
The value proposition
The management team
The competitive advantage
PAUSE: Ask if they have seen other solutions trying to solve the same problem and how your solution stacks up
Progress to date
Current customers
Offer
Call to action
PAUSE: Open the floor to Q&A making sure you ask what their preferred next step is

Figure 7.8   The script.

Source: © Sally Ann Frank

engagement with the participants is much more important than getting through your slide deck.

■ **Boast humbly** – When you get to the "progress to date" section of your presentation, be sure to share all the achievements reached, whether it's regulatory approval, awards, or other extraordinary achievements. In this slide (Figure 7.9) from Hyro, they show their staying power with customers and that they can deliver on the "land and expand" strategy (more on this strategy in Chapter 9) because their customers are satisfied (and probably delighted) with their solution.

Figure 7.9 Boasting humbly.

Source: Hyro pitch deck

■ **Don't let others sell for you** – Only you should be selling your solution. If you have a customer, even a champion, who is representing you at their meetings, prepare to be disappointed. No one should be making your pitch for you with customers. While the decision-making process is often unseen, you should be part of every sales activity until the buying decision is made. If someone offers to sell your solution within their company, politely decline, asking to be included under the direction of the person eager to sell for you. This way, you get a seat at the table, while giving your eager customer a chance to highlight their contribution (and get the recognition, if that's part of their rationale for leading the sales effort). There are times however, that the, "I'll sell it to the team for you," approach is an obfuscation. Instead of admitting to you that the customer doesn't have the authority to make the purchase or the ability to influence the final buying decision, they will offer to make your case, eventually coming back to you with a no-buy decision. *Rarely* does having others sell for you within a customer account work, so do what you can to maintain control of the buying process.

Pitching to Win

One of my favorite "pitchers" is Ronald Steptoe, CEO and co-founder of Warrior Centric Health (WCH), (https://www.warriorcentrichealth.com/) a startup focused on health equity for retired and active military. WCH provides

> solutions that enable healthcare facilities to deliver optimal care to large, diverse populations of patients whose specific needs are now largely overlooked. This includes veterans, active-duty service members, National Guard, reservists, and their families—what we call the Warrior Community. This fully integrated solution suite provides data science to identify these populations, training for staff on how to work within this culture and outreach tools to reach these communities. It's all put into an integrated population health management system that allows health systems, hospitals, and medical centers to get a granular view of who's in their community. We then educate them on how to treat this community effectively, communicate with them, and establish credibility.[1]

In addition to having a real passion for the mission, being a veteran himself and originating from a long, uninterrupted line of veterans going back to the Revolutionary War, Ron's sense of purpose doesn't cloud his ability to pitch the business. I've seen him pitch numerous times, and he never fails to capture the attention of his prospects. He also never fails to provide an offer or next step for customers, and they usually want to take the next step.

I remember one time he was pitching to a retail health organization. After quickly sharing the WCH mission and results to date, he presented a census map of the United States with the locations of active and retired military personnel. On the next slide, he overlaid the retail health locations on the same map and guess what? The stores were in the heart of military communities around the country. Ron and his team had done their home-work and had clearly drawn a line between the WCH solution and a pos-sible new revenue stream for the retailer. And then he went in for the close, showing the pricing structure of the WCH platform, with a special discount for being an early adopter.

Summary

Pitfall	Best Practice
Assuming prospective customers will understand the value of your solution	• Have a clear value proposition • Be ready to customize your pitch for your audience • Remember to suggest a next step, be it an offer to buy or a call to action

Resources

- How to Create Detailed Buyer Personas for Your Business [Free Persona Template] (hubspot.com).
- How to Create a Winning Pitch Deck in Five Steps (forbes.com).
- She's Seen Thousands of Pitch Decks. Here Are the 5 Mistakes Founders Should Avoid (yahoo.com).

Note

1. Warrior Centric Health co-founder Ron Steptoe is on a mission to improve healthcare outcomes for 75 million Americans in the warrior community (microsoft.com).

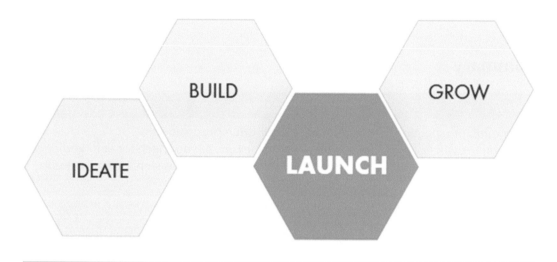

Figure 8.0   Launch.

According to the Oxford Dictionary, "launch" can be defined as "an act or instance of launching something,"[1] "a large motorboat, used especially for short trips," "the largest boat carried on a man-of-war,"[2] "set in motion by pushing it or allowing it to roll into the water,"[3] "set afloat for the first time, typically as part of an official ceremony," "send on its course or into orbit," "start or set in motion,"[4] and "introduce to the public for the first time."[5]

Source: Conversation with Bing, 7/2/2023

(1) https://bing.com/search?q=definition+of+launch.

(2) Launch - definition of launch by The Free Dictionary. https://www.thefreedictionary.com/launch.

(3) Launch Definition & Meaning | Britannica Dictionary. https://www.britannica.com/dictionary/launch.

(4) LAUNCHING | English meaning - Cambridge Dictionary. https://dictionary.cambridge.org/dictionary/english/launching.

(5) Launch Definition & Meaning - Merriam-Webster. https://www.merriam-webster.com/dictionary/launch.

Chapter 8

The Accelerators

Figure 8.1   The accelerators.

Source: © Sally Ann Frank

> *All accelerators are the same. It doesn't matter which one I go through.*

Excited to be accepted into an accelerator program from one of the leading life sciences companies, this particular startup signed all the required documents and attended the kick-off meeting. Meeting the other 11 companies in the cohort, the founder was pleased to see complementary companies participating, instead of competitors. About halfway through the program, it became clear that the goals of the accelerator program were different than the goals of the startup. The startup applied to the accelerator in hopes of closing a small pilot project with the life sciences company. The accelerator program didn't emphasize proof of concepts or pilot projects, but instead,

DOI: 10.4324/9781032639468-8

focused on training programs that would help the startups succeed. Both are admirable objectives, but you can see the mismatch, and so did they. In the end, both the startup and the accelerator agreed to part ways on amicable terms.

But time and resources were wasted on both sides.

Accelerators vary tremendously and selecting the right one (or the wrong one) can have a profound effect on your company and its growth trajectory. But let's start at the beginning; what is an accelerator?

The Accelerator Basics

Startup accelerators support early-stage, growth-driven companies through education, mentorship, and financing. Startups enter accelerators for a fixed-period of time, and as part of a cohort of companies. The accelerator experience is a process of intense, rapid, and immersive education aimed at accelerating the life cycle of young innovative companies, compressing years' worth of learning-by-doing into just a few months.[1]

There are standalone accelerators, like Y Combinator (https://www.ycombinator.com/) and those that are run by corporations, like Merck's MDSS – Accelerating Health & Startups (https://www.mds.studio/) (Microsoft is a partner in the MDSS),[2] or the NHS's NHS Innovation Accelerator, in the UK, (https://nhsaccelerator.com/) or the Cedars Sinai Accelerator (https://csaccelerator.com/) in CA. If you take a moment to review their website, you will see quite different approaches, which reflect their various goals for their accelerator programs.

Let's take a moment to understand the accelerator side of the equation. What do they get out of the deal?

- **Access to innovation** – Especially for the corporate accelerators, this can be a key to developing or maintaining competitive advantage.
- **Monetization of in-house assets** – For corporate accelerators with numerous clinicians, scientists, and other staff members, who are keen to improve the status quo, an accelerator provides a framework for translating an idea from the lab or hospital into a new revenue stream, even if the corporation only maintains a small stake in the new company.

- **Monetization of innovation** – For those accelerators that are independent, make no mistake – the accelerator relationship is a financial one. They are investing time, people, and resources, in exchange for equity in your company that will repay them for their efforts. The investment the accelerator makes varies, as do their expectations of the startups in their programs.
- **Brand cache** – If you are in digital health, you have likely heard of accelerators like Y Combinator or StartUp Health, or others. For corporate accelerators, name recognition, especially when tied to innovation, is important. For those that are not part of a larger corporate entity, they are working to build a name based on successful funding rounds, startups that achieve unicorn status, and startups that have successful exits, all of which draw more top-tier startups to their programs.

If these are the motivations behind accelerators, what factors determine a successful accelerator? Summarizing from Tzahi (Zack) Weisfeld, Vice President, Intel Ignite, (https://www.linkedin.com/in/tweisfeld/), there are three primary variables for corporate accelerators that he outlines in his November 2022 Forbes article:

1. **Staffing** – Minimum of four staffers who themselves have been founders
2. **Budget** – Fully-funded strategic program and not someone's part-time job
3. **Sponsors** – C-level sponsorship for the accelerator[3]

As you investigate accelerator options, keep these three things in mind to ensure that you select an accelerator possessing the wherewithal to support you in your journey. Now that you know a bit more about accelerators and their goals, how do you select one?

The Right Accelerator for You

There are lots of considerations when selecting an accelerator, and there are usually substantial gives and gets between the startup and the accelerator that may go something like what is shown in Figure 8.2.

Accelerator Gives	Accelerator Gets	Startup Gives	Startup Gets
Financial support	Equity	Equity	Participation in accelerator
Training	To know the founder, company, and solution	Time	Apply proven practices
Mentorship	Ability to guide the founding team	Time	1:1 or 1:few personalized guidance to improve chances of success
Networking opportunities	To promote their brand through leading startups	Time	Connections to people who can help you succeed
Co-working space	Organic opportunities to collaborate	Time	Connections with other founders, access to experts, a home office

Figure 8.2   Accelerator and startup gives and gets.

Source: © Sally Ann Frank

When is the right time to join an accelerator? Only you know for sure, but the Silicon Valley Bank (I know, but they have always had terrific information for and about startups) published an extremely helpful article in which they identify the sweet spot for joining an accelerator as, having some customer traction but no outside funding[4]. They even put together a decision tree shown in Figure 8.3, to help founders decide if they are at the right stage to join an accelerator.

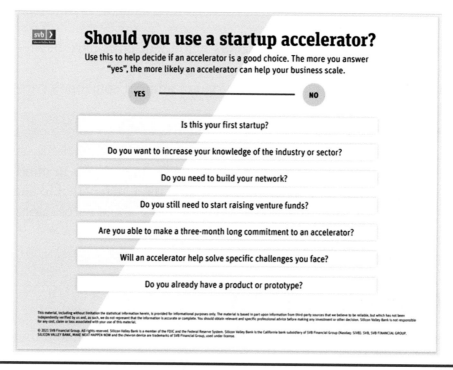

Figure 8.3   Decision process for joining an accelerator.

Source: Silicon Valley Bank, Should You Use a Startup Accelerator? (svb.com)

I generally agree with the "some market traction and no outside funding," time frame, as well. If chosen correctly, the accelerator will help you build upon your customer traction and help you find potential funding sources. Additionally, interest from prospective customers is a key element of what accelerators look for during the application process. Let's dig into the application process, so you know what to expect.

The Correct Fit

Like other important relationships in the life of your startup, finding a good match is important. Before you even complete the application, do some digging on your own to narrow down the options to —three–five accelerators that you would like to consider.

- **Interview accelerator graduates** – Most accelerators have their cohorts listed on their website. Find a company that is adjacent to yours and contact them (via LinkedIn) to get their feedback on the accelerator experience. For example, in Figure 8.4 is a list of companies currently participating in the Merck Digital Sciences Studio accelerator program from their website. If this is an accelerator that you are targeting, you could look at this list, find a company that doesn't compete, and learn about their experience. As the founder of the fictitious AI company, Frank Imaging Solutions, we may want to contact Gesund.ai, a company that is also focused on AI and imaging solutions[5], and see what they have to say about the Merck program.
- **Ensure industry alignment** – Y Combinator is one of the leading accelerators (which bodes well for you, if accepted), but not all industry-agnostic accelerators understand the nuances of the digital health startup journey. Y Combinator has quite a few health tech startups in their portfolio, mostly focused on improving efficiencies in how healthcare is delivered. There are a few that fall into the regulatory realm, but not as many as say Startup + Health, which is dedicated to innovating in healthcare. StartUp Health, established in 2011, has enrolled more than 450 companies in 29 countries.[6]
- **Confirm cultural fit and stage focus** – All organizations have a culture, whether cultivated or not. It will be important to find an accelerator that *feels* right in addition to being a good financial move. You are going to be working with these folks, potentially, well beyond your cohort's program. In addition, if it's a good fit from a cultural perspective, you are more likely to meet other founders who may also become

Meet Our Cohort Companies

The MDS Studio Companies of our First Cohort

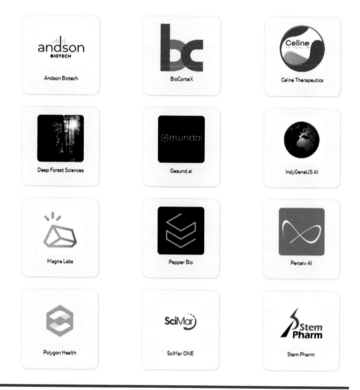

Figure 8.4   Merck Digital Science Studio Cohort.

Source: https://www.mds.studio/companies

valuable connections, colleagues, and even friends. Additionally, making sure that the accelerator you chose (and who choses you) welcomes you at your current stage is key. They have specific resources and programs geared toward startups at a certain stage. Exaggerating customer traction, for example, could land you in an accelerator focused on more mature startups, leaving you unable to take full advantage of the program. Lastly, going back to my conversation with Lisa Maki, and her comment about the four-year lead time for most digital health startups, is also important to consider when evaluating accelerators in addition to funders.

■ **Read their success stories** – Accelerators are always happy to share their latest successes, whether the startup has closed a funding round, been acquired, or achieved some other major milestone. Check their website for their recent news and case studies. Do you see yourself and your company in those stories? If not, then it might not be the right program for you.

■ **Evaluate their community and alumni network** – Most larger accelerators offer programs to companies that have gone through the accelerator. Be sure to investigate what programs are available and if they would be valuable for you.

■ **Understand their positioning** – Knowing their mission, goals, and objectives will help you understand their culture (to some degree) and fit for your company. Here are a few examples to see how each would appeal to a different type of digital health startup:

  – **Y Combinator** – The overall goal of YC is to help startups really take off. They arrive at YC at all different stages. Some haven't even started working yet, and others have been launched for a year or more. But whatever stage a startup is at when they arrive, our goal is to help them to be in dramatically better shape three months later.[7]

  – **StartUp Health** – StartUp Health is the health innovation ecosystem dedicated to achieving health moonshots. We drive sustainable impact through Health Transformer University, our moonshot program designed to help ambitious healthcare founders succeed at every stage.[8]

  – **JLabs (Johnson & Johnson)** – JLABS is a global network of open innovation ecosystems, enabling and empowering innovators across a broad healthcare spectrum including pharmaceutical, medical device, consumer, and health tech sectors to create and accelerate the delivery of life-saving, life-enhancing health, and wellness solutions to patients around the world.[9]

■ **Check out their network** – Most accelerators are eager to play a key role in the startup ecosystem. That typically includes showcasing their network with notable leaders from other parts of the industry. For example, StartUp Health has 1,700 videos on YouTube, including a Fireside Chat playlist with notable industry experts from organizations like 7wireVentures, Amwell, Andreessen Horowitz, and others.[10] (StartUp Health also has videos that cover other helpful topics, so definitely check it out here, https://www.youtube.com/@StartUpHealth/playlists.)

■ **Read the fine print** – Typically, there is some amount of equity or SAFE note tied to participating in the program. Generally, accelerators will take 5–10% of your equity.[11] That's important to know going in and something to keep in mind throughout the application process. If you don't see a TON of value for your 5–10%, then you should find another accelerator program.

■ **Ask about proof of concepts/pilots** – Especially for accelerators that are reflective of your ideal customer (like Cedars Sinai, JLabs, etc.) there should be a pathway to a proof of concept (POC) or pilot project with the company. Be upfront in your desire to take part in the accelerator as a means to getting an opportunity to conduct a small project with them. Not all corporate accelerators offer this, so make sure you know the likelihood (as best as you can) of closing a deal. (More about POCs and pilots in Chapter 9.)

The Application

It's all about the application and finding that right mix of detail, evangelism, and sense of purpose to make your application rise to the top. While the applications typically require you to register first, by digging into the website, you can learn quite a bit about the companies they want to attract. Here are some examples:

■ **Y Combinator** – Requires founders to have 10% ownership, participate in person in San Francisco, and be interviewed virtually as part of the application process.[12]

■ **JLabs** – Specifically states that they are interested in high potential companies in pharmaceuticals, medical devices, consumer health, health tech, and health data science. They even share their selection criteria and exactly what documents they need before you even begin the application.[13]

■ **StartUp Health** – Describes both the process and timeline for applying to their program, which is immensely helpful. They also point applicants to an article on their site that lists the top ten dos and don'ts when applying (which probably works for all accelerators).[14]

■ **Cedars Sinai** – Highlights their key focus areas, enabling you to know immediately if this accelerator is a good choice for you. They list ten different areas, including AI, cybersecurity, genomics, and supply chain management, to name a few.[15]

Lastly, since Microsoft is a partner in the Merck Digital Sciences Studio, I was able to get a list of the questions on the application for the first cohort, launched in October 2022 and shown in Figure 8.5.

Company Background

Company Name

Address

Email

Website

In what state is company registered?

To what location are you applying? [Newark, Cambridge]

When was the company founded?

Founder Details

Founders Names

Founders Titles/Roles

Phone Numbers

Emails

LinkedIn Addresses

Founder Skills

Notable Achievements

What percentage time currently spent at company?

More Company Details

What is your company value proposition?

What is your company mission statement?

How is your company differentiated from current solutions?

Do you currently have contracts or investors?

How much capital have you raised to date, and what sources?

What are your plans to continue raising capital?

What is the ownership structure among company team members?

How many employees currently at the company?

What area is your company most aligned with? Please explain. [Digital Health, Enabling Drug Discovery, Biomarkers, Biomanufacturing, Enabling IT]

Program Information

Why should we select your company?

What three major milestones would you aim to accomplish while in our program?

How are you (or how do you plan to) leverage Microsoft Azure and related resources?

How do you plan to leverage the location and space provided by the program?

How is your company aligned with the program partners (Merck, MSFT, etc.)?

Figure 8.5   MDSS application questions.

Source: Merck Digital Sciences Studio

It's clear to see that answering these questions could take five minutes or many hours. When applying, be concise but clear. In most cases, the reviewers are evaluating hundreds of applications and will choose those that stand out. For example, going back to the fake Frank Imaging Solutions that offers an AI-powered algorithm for detecting pneumonia, Figure 8.6 is an example of how the founder might answer these questions:

What is your company value proposition?

> [Frank Imaging Solutions] helps [clinician] [diagnose pneumonia in seconds] using [AI-powered algorithms that integrate easily into workflows and accelerates treatment].

What is your company mission statement?

> Frank Health puts quick and accurate pneumonia diagnosis and treatment in the hands of clinicians, whether they are in top-rated hospitals or rural clinics.

How is your company differentiated from current solutions?

> Our solution has several important features that differentiate it from others:
>
> - Explainability - It makes recommendations based on explainable AI, enabling the clinician to review the image features that resulted in the diagnosis.
> - Integration – The algorithm seamlessly integrates with workflows and major medical record systems, promoting quick adoption and patient and clinician satisfaction.
> - Validation – We have tested our algorithm with more than 10K patients in the US, Mexico, and India, and have achieved 98% accuracy, focusing more on rural hospitals and clinics, to prove that the solution works in any kind of care setting.
> - Speed to treatment – Our validation studies have shown that patients who have pneumonia are typically treated within hours of their diagnosis, versus days, speeding treatment and needed medication to patients before their condition worsens.

Do you currently have contracts or investors?

> - Contracts – We have validation contracts with hospitals in the US (Cone Health), Mexico (Compañeros En Salud), and India (Acharya Vinoba Bhave Rural Hospital)
> - Investors – We have several angel investors who have invested $750K to date (we can disclose their names after we sign an NDA)

How much capital have you raised to date, and what sources?

> We have raised $750K of angel investing since our inception in 2021 and have runway for another 18 months. After completing this accelerator, we plan to launch our seed round, with a goal of raising $5M. We have started conversations with several potential investors and the general response has been favorable.

What are your plans to continue raising capital?

> We expect that participating in the accelerator will provide additional guidance and connections to investors. As mentioned above, our seed round will be launched while we are in the program or shortly thereafter. Our seed round is slated to be $5M, with our series A of $10M planned for 2025

What is the ownership structure among company team members?

> The founding team consists of 3 people, each with a stake in the company. Our founding team includes Frank Frankenheimer (CEO and co-founder) with 35%, Angelica Juarez, MD, MBA (CRO and co-founder) with 30%, and Devi Patel (CTO and co-founder) with 30%. [Ideally, you would also include LinkedIn profiles, but all of this is fake.] The remaining 5% is owned by our angel investors.

How many employees are currently at the company?

> Our team includes 10 people:
>
> - Founders – 3
> - Engineering – 3
> - AI/ML experts –2
> - Fractional experts – 3
>   i. Regulatory
>   ii. Legal
>   iii. Marketing

Figure 8.6   Completed application.

Source: © Sally Ann Frank

That took me about 15 minutes to write (mostly because I made it up). The bottom line is this, if you want to participate in an accelerator, give the application reviewers the information they need in an easy-to-consume way. Drafting the answers in Word or another document (if possible) enables you to have your founding team or other advisors review and refine your answers, putting your best foot forward. Also, you may be considering several different accelerators. Be sure to respond to each application through the lens from the accelerator itself.

In the above example, we are using questions from the Merck accelerator. If this was a real application for the Merck Digital Sciences Studio, the part "Speed to treatment," would be important because they have a pneumonia vaccine and understanding how Frank Imaging Solutions diagnoses pneumonia could be of value to Merck. Conversely, instead of "Speed to treatment," an accelerator from a provider like Cedars Sinai may also be interested in, "Reducing hospital readmissions." Tying your product to accelerating treatment and reducing hospital admissions or readmissions is likely to be more important to them, so in this case, you may opt to mention both.

Especially for first time founders, accelerators are a valuable way to infuse the company with direction, best practices, and practical advice. "[A]ccelerators *can* have a positive effect on the performance of the start-ups they work with, even compared with other key early-stage investors. But this finding is not universal among all accelerators and so far has been isolated to leading programs. Early evidence also shows that accelerators may have a positive effect on attracting seed and early-stage financing to a community, bringing spillover benefits to the wider regional economy."[16]

Summary

Pitfall	Best Practice
Not conducting due diligence on accelerators	• Do the research and find an accelerator that suits your company mission, goals, and culture • Participate fully in the program and if you can't commit, then wait until you can • Know what you are getting into regarding the program, the financials, and the benefits

Resources

- Starting a Corporate Startup Accelerator? Here's How to Make It a Success (forbes.com).
- How Do Startup Accelerators Work? | Silicon Valley Bank (svb.com).
- 100 Startup Accelerators around the World – Crunchbase.
- I've Vetted 3,000 Health Startups: Here Are 10 Things I Wish Every Founder Knew | by StartUp Health | StartUp Health (healthtransformer.co).

Notes

1. What Startup Accelerators Really Do (hbr.org).
2. Merck Announces the Launch of the Merck Digital Sciences Studio to Help Healthcare Startups Quickly Bring their Innovations to Market – Merck.com.
3. Starting a Corporate Startup Accelerator? Here's How to Make It a Success (forbes.com).
4. How Do Startup Accelerators Work? | Silicon Valley Bank (svb.com).
5. MDSS – Gesund.ai.
6. StartUp Health Portfolio – StartUp Health.
7. About Y Combinator | Y Combinator.
8. StartUp Health.
9. Vision | JLABS (jnjinnovation.com).
10. Fireside Chats – YouTube.
11. How Do Startup Accelerators Work? | Silicon Valley Bank (svb.com).
12. Apply to Y Combinator | Y Combinator.
13. JLABS Resident Application (smapply.io).
14. Founders: Apply to Health Transformer University – StartUp Health.
15. Apply – Cedars-Sinai Accelerator (csaccelerator.com).
16. What Startup Accelerators Really Do (hbr.org).

Chapter 9

The GTM Strategies

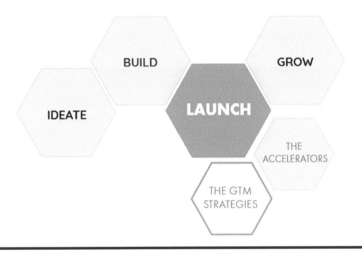

Figure 9.1   The GTM Strategies.

If I build it, they will come.

I have spoken to many founders about their go-to-market strategies (GTMs), and many others who had no plan or strategy whatsoever. I remember meeting with a founder with a very niche solution for helping patients develop healthier eating habits by connecting them with registered dieticians and nutritionists. When pressed, he couldn't tell me if he was targeting consumers directly or organizations like medical practices and hospitals. He had a mobile phone app that he was developing and that's all he had thought about. He had fallen into the classic trap of putting the product ahead of everything else. He hadn't done any customer discovery, competitive

DOI: 10.4324/9781032639468-9

analysis, business model development, or GTM strategy. He had an app. End of story. End of company.

According to Hubspot, the four main elements of a go-to-market (GTM) strategy are:

- Product-market fit
- Target audience
- Competition and demand
- Distribution[1]

That same article has a few templates that you may also find helpful, and you'll find it listed in the resources section at the end of this chapter. But before diving into the go-to-market (GTM) strategy, let's quickly review some of the GTM elements that we've already covered in Figure 9.2.

Element	Defined	Cross reference
Product-market fit	Mission, value proposition & solution	Chapters 1, 2, 4, and 6
Target audience	Personas and titles	Chapter 7
Competition and demand	TAM and competitors	Chapter 5 and 7
Distribution	Alternatives to direct selling	This chapter

Figure 9.2 GTM elements.

Source: © Sally Ann Frank

While we have covered most of these elements in terms of the funding and customer pitch, let's go to the next level and discuss these elements in terms of the GTM strategy. Specifically, we will move from describing these elements to how you execute each one.

Product-Market Fit

Let's start with the term "product-market fit." According to Marc Andreessen, co-founder of Andreessen Horowitz, "product/market fit means being in a good market with a product that can satisfy that market."[2] That same article, shares this definition from Andy Rachleff, from Wealthfront and former co-founder of VC firm Benchmark Capital:

> A value hypothesis is an attempt to articulate the key assump-
> tion that underlies why a customer is likely to use your product.

Identifying a compelling value hypothesis is what I call finding product/market fit. A value hypothesis identifies the features you need to build, the audience that's likely to care, and the business model required to entice a customer to buy your product. Companies often go through many iterations before they find product/market fit if they ever do." "When a great team meets a lousy market, market wins. When a lousy team meets a great market, market wins. When a great team meets a great market, something special happens." "If you address a market that really wants your product – if the dogs are eating the dog food – then you can screw up almost everything in the company and you will succeed. Conversely, if you're really good at execution but the dogs don't want to eat the dog food, you have no chance of winning.

Regardless of which definition you like, there is a common theme – what you are building must fulfill a market need. For founders in digital health, perhaps more so than in other industries, often the concept for a solution or company comes from personal experience, seeing an unmet need or a realization that a care pathway, or workstream, or other aspect of healthcare can be improved. And you believe you are the catalyst for change.

I know many digital health startups established by clinicians, scientists, and patients, and their stories and raison d'être are truly inspiring. I shared Liz O'Day's story in the preface, about how she witnessed the difficulties her older brother had, as he was fighting (and ultimately overcame) childhood cancer. So profoundly affected by the experience, she dedicated her life and livelihood to making treatment easier for other patients and launched Olaris (https://www.myolaris.com/), based on the work she conducted while earning her PhD from Harvard.

Another example is Dock Health (https://www.dock.health/). Frustrated by the lack of consistency when treating patients, it was co-founded by Michael Docktor, MD (yes, that is his real name), pediatric gastroenterologist and former clinical director of innovation at Boston Children's Hospital and Nitin Gujral, former director of Innovation and R&D at Boston Children's Hospital. Here's more information about their origin story from their website:

We were founded to help solve a fundamental problem we experienced ourselves as providers, the gap between the clinical intent and all the administrative work required to ensure a patient's needs are delivered upon. As a pediatric gastroenterologist and clinical director of innovation at Boston Children's Hospital, Michael Docktor faced this problem daily. He wanted the best for his patients but there were too many balls in the air, too many administrative tasks he had to track and no good way to reliably work with his team or ensure all the loops were closed. He was inspired by the collaborative yet simple, shared to-do list he used with his wife to manage their food shopping list and wondered, "How does this not exist in healthcare?"

Like Dock Health, RxLightning (https://www.rxlightning.com/) is automating manual workflows and streamlining the process of specialty medication management. Co-founders Julia Regan (CEO) and Brad Allen (CTO) were both involved in the digital health ecosystem, having worked together at a healthcare data processing and support company. Additionally, Julia had worked in the pharmaceutical industry, and both were keenly aware of the antiquated, slow process of prescribing and managing specialty medications. Often these life-saving drugs were taking months to grind through the very manual approval process, using faxes and other outdated technology. Together, Julia and Brad are changing the system from the inside, accelerating treatment for patients in an impactful way. Furthermore, the pharmaceutical companies and providers are enthusiastic about RxLightning's ability to improve patient care.

Peter Kim, MD, is on a mission to update and improve surgical procedures, through his company, Activ Surgical (https://www.activsurgical.com/). Their mission is clearly stated on their website, "Our mission is for every surgical imaging system to deliver intelligent information that reduces surgical complication rates, ushering in a new standard of patient care and safety."[3] As a pediatric surgeon, he was driven to improve outcomes. In his words:

"Innovation in the surgical vision category is long overdue; the most commonly employed surgical imaging process, ICG, uses fluorescent dye invented more than 70 years ago and does not offer real-time, objective physiologic information to surgeons when they critically need it during procedures," said Dr. Peter Kim, co-founder and chief science officer, Activ Surgical. "Activ Surgical is designed to empower surgeons to make better informed decisions by offering real-time intelligence and visualization to dramatically reduce medical complications and surgical errors."[4]

Inspiring origin stories are just the beginning when it comes to product-market fit. Just because you see a need, doesn't mean that there is enough market potential to build a *successful* company. In previous chapters, we have addressed the solution, technology, company, and the pitches, both for VCs and customers. Based on all the work to date, you should be able to surmise if you have a problem worth solving and if customers will buy. There is no heuristic that states, "if you ask 10 people if they would buy your solution, and 7 say yes, then you have a good product." However, if you have been diligent about your customer discovery, connections with potential investors, and technology infrastructure to build it, then you are on the right track.

The hardest part about achieving product-market fit is to take off your rose-colored glasses and see your company, solution, and GTM strategy from a customer's perspective. Unfortunately, I have seen far too many founders with ideas that will never achieve product-market fit for their digital health solution. Why? There are a variety of reasons, of course, but many of them are related to an overblown sense of their own abilities to overcome obstacles, or refusal to recognize the obstacles. Furthermore, while I'm a fan of dreaming big, many founders are going for "moon shots," which can lead to long cycles that ultimately lead to failure. Moon shots aren't bad, but a moon shot without baby steps is destined to fail, because product-market fit could be years away. Instead, identify your moon shot, but then build deliverable portions of that moon shot along the way.

Think about Covid-19 for a moment. Was the initial plan to eradicate the virus from the population (moon shot)? No, the first step was to fast-track a shot regimen that lessened the severity of the disease. If you are building your company based on a moon shot, consider portions of that journey, and find ways to package and sell incremental products that bring value to your business and customers along the way.

Confirming Product Market Fit

Once you have done your research and believe that there is a place for your solution in the industry, it's time to do some additional validation. In Chapter 1, we talked about using interviews, polls, and research to confirm that the problem is really a problem and worth solving. To confirm product-market fit, we must build on those findings, using a prototype or perhaps an MVP.

Start by going back to those —five–ten proxy customers that you interviewed and show them what you've built. Leave your ego behind, and listen, *really listen* to what they are telling you. If they are willing to, record the conversation so that you can refer to their exact words repeatedly. (And if you use Microsoft Teams and record the call, the AI tool will take the notes and summarize them for you!) Be ready to evolve your thinking, especially when it comes to the user interface, interoperability requirements, and workflow integration. Consider sharing some preliminary information before you meet with your proxy customers. Often a brief video (~3 minutes or less), a quick overview, or even your website will help set the stage for your meeting.

Be sure to ask your proxy customers open-ended questions once you get past the buy/not buy question. This simple decision tree in Figure 9.3 is an example of how you might architect the discussion. Note the bottom path, where the proxy customers say that they wouldn't buy your

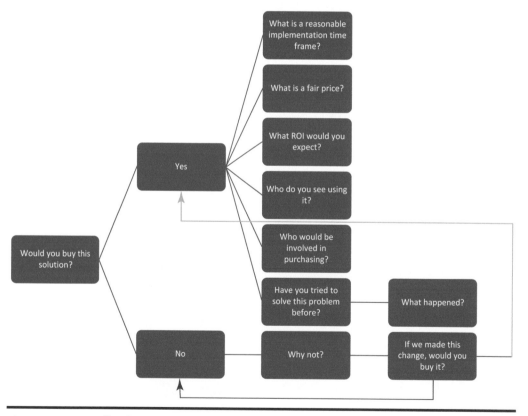

Figure 9.3 Confirming product market fit.

Source: © Sally Ann Frank

solution. Respond with a couple of reasonable changes to your approach, perhaps even suggested by them, and ask the question again. If you continue that cycle two–three times and the answer is still no, then it's time to move on. Either to a different customer interview or a new business, depending on if that detractor was in the majority or minority of your interviewees.

And now you are done, right? Not exactly. Conduct the same interviews with prospective investors, those who you've been cultivating and following on social media, asking them if they would invest instead of buy.

Keep in mind, if you have the funding, there are tons of companies out there that would love to do this empirical market research for you, like Design Map, (https://designmap.com/), Cambridge Design Partnership (https://www.cambridge-design.com/), and The Abed Graham Group (https://www.abedgraham.com/) (these are not endorsements, just options). Your chosen accelerator may also have good options for you in this area.

If you've gotten to the point that you have an MVP, there is no better way to get confirmation and refinement of your solution than to find a few customers who are eager to evaluate your MVP. A lot goes into testing an MVP (which could be an entirely separate book), but in digital health, it's important to ensure that patient care isn't affected when assessing the MVP.

For example, instead of running the MVP on the customer's data and in their infrastructure, you could opt to use a public data set like one of these on your own cloud instance.

- Microsoft https://learn.microsoft.com/en-us/azure/open-datasets/dataset -catalog
- AWS https://aws.amazon.com/marketplace/search/results?trk=868d8747 -614e-4d4d-9fb6-fd5ac02947a8&sc_channel=el&FULFILLMENT_OPTION _TYPE=DATA_EXCHANGE&CONTRACT_TYPE=OPEN_DATA_ LICENSES&filters=FULFILLMENT_OPTION_TYPE%2CCONTRACT_TYPE
- Google https://research.google/resources/datasets/
- NIH (US) https://sharing.nih.gov/accessing-data
- NHS (UK) https://digital.nhs.uk/data-and-information/data-collections -and-data-sets/data-sets

Alternatively, you could use synthetic data sets like the one from Humana (https://developers.humana.com/syntheticdata, or anonymize data using a solution from a company like Private.AI (https://www.private-ai.com/), a data security startup that enables organizations to "detect, anonymize, and replace 50+ entities of personally identifiable information in 49 languages with better accuracy than big tech."[5]

Typically, once you have an MVP, you are likely to go through a series of steps that help you move to product-market fit, including proof of concepts, clinical validation, and pilot projects.

Proof of Concepts

Ideally, you should have an MVP architecture built that fosters quick and easy proof of concepts (POCs) to be conducted without risk to your customer. This is part of the alignment of your product roadmap, regulatory journey, and go-to-market strategy that we discussed in Chapter 6.

And to be clear, a POC is literally a proof of concept, i.e., you are proving the efficacy of your solution in a controlled environment and without directly affecting patient care. Instead use existing data sets, anonymized data, or other means to replicate how your solution would be used. Once you have proven the technology works, you may need to also conduct clinical validation, especially if your solution is designed to improve clinical outcomes or provide clinical decision support.

Clinical Validation

After the POC, you will likely move to clinical validation. Clinical validation

> can be defined as demonstrating theclinical safety, effectiveness, and efficacy. Safety illustrates that the product [has] minimal chance for error or adverse effect to the patient. Effectiveness reflects how reproducible the product is in delivering benefit in the real world, whilst efficacy captures the degree to which the product performs its role well.[6]

Typically, a startup would engage with a validation partner, like an Academic Medical Center (AMC) or other healthcare organization, and pay researchers to do an actual clinical trial on the solution.[7] The Taylor & Francis group, has a helpful, in-depth article about the process of clinical validation, Digital Health; What Do We Mean by Clinical Validation? (tandfonline.com) that is also referenced by Pubmed.[8]

Pilots

Once your clinical validation is completed, your likely next step is a pilot, which is more valuable for both you and your customer, is a small-scale implementation of your *entire* solution, which implies that you have moved beyond MVP. If you are on the cusp of or at product-market fit, always opt for the pilot, as it sets you up for clinical validation followed by a land-and-expand approach.

Land and Expand

Land and expand is nirvana for a business of any size. It is the strategy of starting with a small initial deal (pilot) to build credibility and affinity and then transitioning to larger sales. For example, our AI-powered pneumonia company may start by conducting a small pilot in one hospital and then move into others within the hospital system. In fact, Cynerio (https://www.cynerio .com/), a healthcare-focused cybersecurity company, prevents attacks from impacting patients, facilities, and their finances. By focusing on connected devices "attack detection, risk mediation prioritization, and long-term security protection,"[9] Cynerio has managed to execute on this land and expand approach. With a global focus, Cynerio's recent collaboration with several NHS Trusts quickly expanded to several dozen as a combination of current regulatory requirements and cybersecurity vision paved the way for success.

Another successful "lander and expander" is Hyro (https://www.hyro.ai/), the conversational AI company mentioned in Chapter 2. They are masterful at starting by solving a single problem and then using their success to move into other use cases for their customers. In 2022, Hyro began working with Baptist Health North Florida on a very specific problem – dealing with increased calls to the service desk. In this case, Baptist Health was gearing up for an Epic implementation and expected that they would receive an increased volume of calls to the service desk. "Baptist Health's adoption of Hyro's adaptive, language-based AI assistants is helping to offload repetitive tasks such as password resets from Baptist team members and allow more time for them to focus on value-add services."[10] Brilliant, right? Furthermore, Baptist Health was able to "experience value in as little at 10 days."[11] You can expect (as the team at Hyro will ensure) that this small, highly successful implementation will grow and expand to additional departments across the five-hospital system.

Leverage Early Adopters

I'm a fan of early adopter programs, and they are especially fitting for digital health startups to help manage the long product development and revenue timeline. According to Hubspot,

> Early adopters are the first customers to adopt a new product or technology before the majority of the population does. They're often called "lighthouse customers" because they serve as a beacon of light for the rest of the population to follow, which will take the technology or product mainstream.[12]

This is a helpful baseline, but in digital health early adopter programs should be slightly different.

When I think of early adopters in the context of healthcare and life sciences startups, I think about validation partners, IRBs, and possibly clinical trials. Early adopters are organizations and customers who will collaborate with you to generate the data needed for regulatory clearance. For those solutions that don't require regulatory clearance, as well as those that do, early adopter programs are helpful in building marketing assets that can be used to promote your startup.

For example, BeekeeperAI (https://www.beekeeperai.com/), a startup that uses Azure confidential computing and privacy preserving analytics for the training, validation, and deployment of artificial intelligence (AI) in healthcare, was a spin-off from University of California San Francisco (UCSF), with UCSF as their first customer.

> By incubating BeeKeeperAI within CDHI [Center for Digital Health], the founding team had direct access to a variety of experts in data science, clinical informatics, medical care, product development, and data stewardship. Early efforts included extensive market fit testing that led to a robust pipeline of initial data stewards and algorithm developers.[13]

However, your startup may not be a spin-out, so you will need to think differently about early adopters. You will have to find your own early adopters through connections you or your team members have. The early adopters can be any of the personas and titles mentioned in Chapter 7, but they need to be a *special* kind of person. TechTarget.com, in an article penned by Rahul Awati, describes early adopters this way:

> Early adopters differ from the other adopter categories in their willingness to support new ideas, try new things and embrace change. They're not averse to taking risks and are among the first to adopt and use an innovation and provide feedback about their experience.
>
> Early adopters like to do things others are unwilling to do, either due to fear or skepticism about the product or disdain for any new technology. By taking such risks, they influence the development and enhancement of new technology and often become opinion leaders and social influencers. In those roles, they help others – followers – decide whether they'd also like to try the product.[14]

There are a few key phrases in Awati's description: "not averse to taking risks," "become opinion leaders and social influencers," and help followers "decide whether they'd also like to try the product." These phrases are clues to who you should seek when trying to find the right early adopter. However, finding enthusiasm for change in a laggard industry like healthcare and life sciences can be exceedingly difficult. Develop a balanced plan, relying both on your team's network of contacts and social media to find the right influencers. Another option is to work with organizations that are keen to be on the front lines of innovation in digital health, like Inflect Health or the American Medical Association.

Inflect Health, part of Vituity (https://www.vituity.com/), serves as an innovation hub.

> As part of Vituity, Inflect Health has access to thousands of doctors, clinicians, and key industry stakeholders. This access allows Inflect Health to not only provide investment, *but also first-hand development support by connecting innovators to physicians and patients in real-time.* [emphasis added] This unique approach to investment and support increases the opportunity for success and continues to strengthen Vituity's history of healthcare transformation.[15]

Essentially, Inflect Health will provide validation services, which they have offered to several startups that I know.

Additionally, the American Medical Association as the AMA Physician Innovation Network (PIN) (https://innovationmatch.ama-assn.org/), is designed to match physicians with early-stage companies to foster and accelerate innovation. This program could open the door for early adopters, especially if your startup aligns with their goals, outlined below in Figure 9.4.

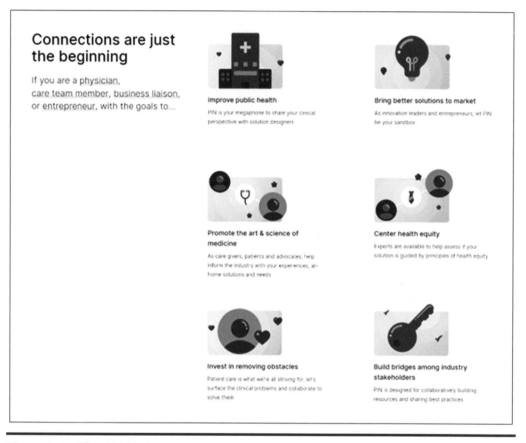

Figure 9.4   The AMA's PIN.

Source: © 2023 American Medical Association. All rights reserved. Used with permission.

It's clear that an early adopter program can be highly beneficial for start-ups, but what do the early adopters get? Figure 9.5 a potential list of gives and gets from both side of the equation.

As a founder, you are clearly passionate about solving the problem you have selected as the foundation for your company. Make sure that your prospective early adopters share your passion at the same intensity (or close to it). Early adopter programs are terrific when they work well. If you have started working with someone who doesn't share your vision or passion, your chances of a successful relationship diminish greatly.

Early Adopter Gives	Startup Gets	Startup Gives	Early Adopter Gets
Opinions and feedback of the product	Unvarnished input from a user who matches targeted personas	Access to new technology	Ability to test new technology
Referrals to others who may be interested as early adopters	Multiple data points	Recognition as an early adopter	Ability to add new skills and be a thought leader
Public acknowledgement of the partnership	A customer logo to add to their GTM	Access to findings (in compliance with regulations), if more than one early adopter is participating	Additional data points on how the solution can be used and the results
Documented case study (assuming the project is a success)	A customer story to use in GTM activities and on their website	Ability to publish a white paper, research, or other scholarly document	Opportunity to participate in a meaningful research project

Figure 9.5   Early adopter gives and gets.

Source: © Sally Ann Frank

Validation to Production

Even as you are identifying your validation partner or partners, you need to map out the process for your early adopters to move from validation to production. Not every validation partner will end up as production win, but establishing a pathway for that progression enables you to move things along with your validation partner and identify points along the way where you can add others who want to join the journey. Looking at the chart in Figure 9.6 below, you can see how you could easily begin the journey at any point along the continuum from validation to production.

When building this journey, there are a couple of important caveats you should consider, both of which deal with the economics of pricing.

- **Free** – Unless you are specifically offering a freemium version of your product, free is never a good option for anything but validation. In fact, if your prospective customer is not willing to cover your costs for a proof of concept, then, as hard as it is, walk away. Either you've not conveyed the value, or your proxy customers didn't understand of the actual market value or both. Regardless, if you are haggling at this point, then this customer may not be a good choice for you. Firing prospects and customers is the hardest thing a company leader must do, but it will save you tons of headaches (and unrecouped costs) in the long run.

Validation
- Stage: Prototype or MVP
- Price: No cost for validation partner
- Goal: Validation that solution can solve the problem
- Startup value: Additional fine-tuning of solution, possible marketing material

POC
- Stage: MVP
- Price: At cost
- Goal: Prove the solution works as intended and solves the problem
- Startup value: Paying customer, possible customer story

Pilot
- Stage: MVP or Product-market fit
- Price: Small margin
- Goal: Prove that the entire solution works as intended, within a small implementation
- Startup value: Paying customer, possible customer story, runway to full production win

Production
- Stage: Product-market fit
- Price: Larger margin
- Goal: Prove that the entire solution works as intended, at scale
- Startup value: Paying customer, possible customer story, win to leverage with other prospects

Figure 9.6   Validation to production.

Source: © Sally Ann Frank

■ **Rebates** – One of the strategies I've always liked is to offer rebates if someone moves from pilot to production. The table in Figure 9.7 could be a possible scenario.

Price of pilot	$25K
Price of production implementation	$295K
Total price	$320K
Minus rebate*	($15K)
Final price	$305K

Rebate applied when contract is signed along with an agreement to issue a press release about the production implementation and a joint customer story

Figure 9.7   Rebate scenario.

Source: © Sally Ann Frank

Now, $305K is an odd number, so if you find yourself in negotiations, it's easy to drop the price to an even $300K. Remember, customers will try to negotiate on price. Have your pricing strategy, and what you are willing to give up, ready for the final discussions. You may be willing to give up some cash, or the announcement of the partnership, but I would caution you to avoid giving up the customer story in final negotiations. If you are successful and they are amenable to a case study, there is no better piece of marketing collateral.

Target Audience

In Chapter 7, we discussed the personas and titles you intend to target. You know who they are, but how do you reach them? There are many ways to connect with your target audience, and the resources at the end of this chapter list some terrific books to help you. I strongly urge you to read those books, but for our purposes, we will summarize ways to connect with your target audience, which in broad terms include in-person and virtual.

- **In-person industry events** – It's always easier, especially when you are an early-stage company, to go where your customers already are. That means industry events; however, it may not be the big industry events that are the most beneficial for you. To start, consider smaller, specialized events, instead of HIMSS (https://www.himss.org) or DIA (https://www.diaglobal.org/), as it's often hard to get mindshare with 40K+ people mulling about. Personally, I have found HLTH (https://www.hlth.com/) and ViVE (https://www.viveevent.com/) to be very helpful for many of the startups I work with, but other, more focused ones could also be more beneficial than the larger conferences. I know startups that attend:
  - SCOPE – Summit For Clinical Ops Executives (scopesummit.com)
  - AHIP Conferences – AHIP
  - American Society of Cataract and Refractive Surgery | ASCRS
  - Becker's Upcoming Conferences (beckershospitalreview.com)
  - Events – ATA (americantelemed.org)
  - Radiological Society of North America | RSNA
  - 2023 USA | RSA Conference

  It's important to note that it's one thing to attend, and another to present. Whenever possible, apply to speak at these events. Typically, show organizers like to see presentations that include customers as well as the startup, turning the session into a true thought leadership presentation versus a sales presentation. At an American Society of Cataract and Refractive Surgery (ASCRS) annual meeting in May 2023, Microsoft hosted a startup symposium where 12 startups from our program presented to the conference attendees. The attendees were in-person, while some startups presented in-person and others were virtual (one founder presented at 3am his time!). As a result of this event, 4 out of the 12 startups have ongoing engagements with prospects they met at the event. (You can check out recordings of the pitches here, https:// ascrs.org/clinical-education/presentations-on-demand/meetings/2023 -ascrs-annual-meeting/sessions/2023-microsoft.)

Many of these events include their own platform for networking. I have found, however, that few of the people you really want to meet at these events are active on those networks. I've come up with a workaround that's been effective for me:

1. **Search** – Find the person you would like to meet on the event networking site, based on company, title, or person's name to confirm they are attending.
2. **Use LinkedIn** – Send a connection request (not inMail) with a brief description of why you want to meet with them. Only 300 characters are allowed in the connection message, so you must be concise. Your connection message might be:

Hello [customer first name], Based on your posts, we have common areas of interest, specifically in [topic y] and [topic z]. If you are also going to [event name], I'd love to meet to discuss trends and innovations in these areas. Please email at name@company.com, so we can set something up. Thank you.

That is less than 300 characters, leaving you a few extra characters. The magic of this method is that they immediately go to your LinkedIn profile and can see that you are a real person and innovator, with similar interests. It doesn't work 100%, but hopefully you will be pleasantly surprised at how well it does work (as some of the startups I work with have noted).

■ **In-person bespoke events** – For companies of all sizes, getting invited by a customer to present at an event they are hosting for their organization is the best way to engage with your target audience and prospects. These are definitely harder to come by, but as part of my work, I help corporate customers organize "innovation days," in which some of the startups in my portfolio are asked to take part with pitches, participate in panel discussions, or staff mini-booths with demos and other information. It's not uncommon for five–seven startups to participate, with a couple moving onto the next step of deeper discussions about a proof of concept or pilot project. And while this is much more effective as an in-person event (mostly due to additional networking opportunities that are available), they can be done virtually as well, especially when the customer and startups are geographically dispersed. The key to being invited to these is to use existing customers (champions), partners, proxy customers, and other members of the tribe to help you uncover these opportunities.

▪ **Sales Navigator** – Another part of LinkedIn that you should consider is Sales Navigator. (Microsoft for Startups offers licenses to LinkedIn with access to Sales Navigator to startups in the startup program.) Regardless of what technology you are using, Sales Navigator (Figure 9.8) has tremendous tools to support your GTM for in-person and virtual connections. You can enter target personas, track accounts and leads, and even post content with a SmartLink that will allow you to track who opens the content, without them having to enter their email or any other information.

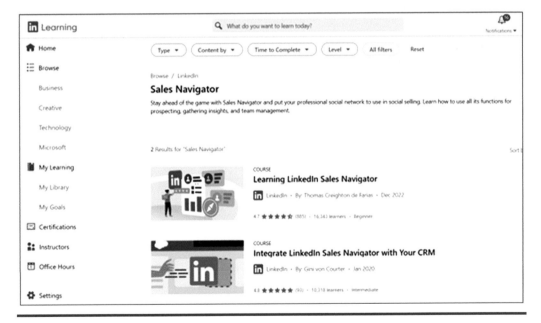

Figure 9.8   Sales Navigator.

Source: Sales Navigator: Online Courses, Training and Tutorials on LinkedIn Learning https://www .linkedin.com/learning/topics/sales-navigator?u=3322.

- **LinkedIn marketing campaigns** – LinkedIn has a rich set of marketing tools to help you attract your target audience and has several articles that outline best practices for marketing on their platform, including:
  - How to Create a LinkedIn Advertising Campaign | LinkedIn Ads
    - https://business.linkedin.com/marketing-solutions/success/best -practices/create-your-first-campaign
  - 10 Examples of LinkedIn Ads That Totally Crushed It
    - https://www.linkedin.com/business/marketing/blog/linkedin-ads /10-examples-of-linkedin-ads-that-totally-crushed-it
  - Unlock Your Campaign's Potential with LinkedIn's New A/B Testing
    - https://www.linkedin.com/business/marketing/blog/linkedin-ads/ linkedin-ads-new-ab-testing-features

In many cases, LinkedIn marketing campaigns can be cost-effective, easy-to-launch programs for testing out messaging, while giving you the ability to finely-tune who is in your target audience. As your company grows and your messaging becomes more refined, there are likely to be additional marketing channels you will want to investigate, but LinkedIn is a great place to start.

Following Up

These strategies all require a certain amount of follow up, typically done by email. Email is tremendously easy as a method of communications when you are in sales mode, but it's also the easiest for your prospect to ignore. I've developed a few methods of making sure follow up activities are effective that I will share with you.

- **Add value** – Have you ever gotten an email (or several) that said, "Just following up on our meeting to see if you want to discuss the project further…" Ugh. Instead, bring additional value to the interaction by sharing an article or new piece of information. Try this instead, "I wanted to share this article from Becker's with you, because it highlights the problem that I believe we can help you solve…" Much better, right?
- **Pick up the phone** – I had a colleague who used to say, "If you have emailed more than three times about something, make a phone call." Phone calls can also be ignored, but I have a suggestion there, too.

Make the call, leave a voicemail, and *then* email as well. While this does come dangerously close to stalking (not really, but you know what I mean), the combination of a quick voicemail and subsequent email says you are serious. And if you add value in the voicemail or email, even better.

Social Media

Social media is another way to draw (hopefully positive) attention to you and your company, if you do it correctly. Social media can include posts to platforms like LinkedIn, as well as blogs that you can publish on your website or as an article on LinkedIn. However, there are a few caveats to consider before you start your social media approach:

▪ **Don't start what you can't sustain**. This is especially important for early-stage companies. Nothing is more disheartening for a prospective customer or funder than to go to a website and see that they've not posted a blog or an update in months (or years). Instead of pledging to post a blog a week, try once a month. Alternatively, set up a schedule where each member of the leadership team writes a blog per quarter. This way each of you shares responsibility and is not overwhelmed. (You can also have people ghost-write blogs, but I've not seen that be terribly successful, as you end up spending as much time with the ghost-writer as you would if you did it yourself.) Don't forget to consider using ChatGPT to move things along. As startup Cynerio recently posted in a press release, "This press release drafted by ChatGPT, perfected by humans."[16]

▪ **It's as much about what you don't post**. Personally, I like to see startups and their leaders post about their company, solutions, customers, issues, and trends that are affecting them. If you want to share your latest vacation or an achievement of a family member, consider doing that on Facebook or Instagram. As an early-stage company, you are posting to build your brand and anything that is not "on brand" will dilute your messaging and diminish your impact. Once you have established yourself, you can widen the topics that you post about, but that decision should come much, much later. Lastly, ChatGPT can also help with social posts, making the process easier and faster. (I do this quite a bit myself.)

■ **Make it easy to share**. For each blog you post, be sure to add the ability to share that link to social channels. Use the icons for LinkedIn, Twitter, and other platforms on the side or bottom of your blog posts to make them easy to share.

Competition

One of my biggest challenges with founders is their belief that their solution is unique, and they have no competition. This usually means that the startup team hasn't done the proper research recommended in Chapters 1, 2, 6, and 7. There is *always* competition and perhaps the most overlooked competitor is "doing nothing." Don't forget that when competing against inertia, you must prove to your customer that your solution is worth the investment to change what they are doing and endure potential disruption to operations (no matter how slight), and that it will generate the ROI you claim.

One of my favorite ways to compete with inertia is to develop an ROI calculator. Similar to many of the ROI calculators for financial instruments, the ROI calculator is designed to convey the value of investing in your solution. Instead of pure financial gain, an ROI calculator can show time saved, money saved, improved throughput, increased revenue, or several other metrics that are important to your prospects. SciMar One (https://scimarone.com) works with pharmaceutical companies to improve their "Development Velocity," described as "the speed a pharmaceutical company moves therapies from the lab, through development, and into the market."[17] Not only have they developed an ROI calculator, they have also put it on their website, to help everyone immediately understand the SciMar One value proposition. You can check it out at https://scimarone.com/dv-estimator/.

When telling your story within the competitive landscape, it's important to be respectful (never trash another company), metric-based, accurate, and consistent. Furthermore, if you can get someone else to do the research for you, even better. CB Insights generates annual lists of the top startups in certain technology and industry areas.

Hyro, the conversational AI company mentioned earlier, was able to secure a spot in the CB Insights Digital Health 150 for 2022. Nothing says, "we are a leader in this space," like being selected out of 13,000 private companies who vied for one of the coveted 150 spots in 2022.

You may be asking why competition is part of the GTM strategy. It's because you must be prepared to respond to questions from prospects when they ask, "Why are you better than solution X?" In fact, you may find that you are consistently coming up against a single competitor. In that case, not only should you be prepared to answer questions, but you may also want to build an entire messaging strategy for that single competitor. For example, Cynerio, a cybersecurity startup with a mission, "to secure every IoT, IoMT, OT and IT device in healthcare,"[18] was perceived as being competitive with Microsoft Sentinel, which was especially problematic when trying to sell their solution into Microsoft accounts with Microsoft account teams. Instead of continuing the battle, they did some technical and market work and in June 2023, "announced its collaboration with Microsoft to integrate with their cloud-native SIEM and SOAR offering Microsoft Sentinel. This collaboration aims to provide the healthcare industry with a comprehensive solution to address the growing security challenges posed by medical and IoT devices."[19] In other words, they removed the perceived competition by integrating their solution with the Microsoft offering and then announcing it.

Distribution

Which brings us to distribution and channel partners. As a small company, direct sales can be a slow path to growth, until the large amounts of funding come in and you can hire a sales team. That is why finding and collaborating with key partners can be a helpful strategy to accelerate growth. There are several types of partnerships with these likely to be the most common:

- **Systems integrators** – Large systems integration or consulting partners can be extremely helpful, especially in the first few years of your company. Not only can these organizations help you sell, they can also help with deployment services, customer support, and marketing. The potential downside is that they build their own solution based on their experience with you. But that hasn't stopped many startups from setting up these partnerships. In the case of Well-Beat (https://www.well-beat .com/), a solution that empowers healthcare providers and organizations to dramatically increase patient engagement and treatment regime adherence,[20] they not only partnered with UST, but also received investment from the systems integrator.[21]
- **Channel partners** – Many would consider AWS, GCP, and Microsoft to be channel partners, as these partnership relationships are largely based

on using the cloud technology and then parlaying that relationship into co-marketing and co-selling activities. In Chapter 4, when discussing the technology, we covered the startup programs, investment arms, and partner program for each major cloud vendor. In Figure 9.9, we add their marketplaces, which enable startups and other external partners to sell their solutions through these commerce sites.

Cloud	Marketplace	Startup program	Investment Arm	Partner Program
AWS	https://aws.amazon.com/market place/	https://aws.amazon.com/startups/	Various investment funds	AWS Partner Network
GCP	https://cloud.google.com/market place/	https://cloud.google.com/startup	Google Ventures	Google Partners
Microsoft Azure	https://azuremarketplace.microso ft.com/en-us/marketplace/	https://www.microsoft.com/en-us/startups	M12	Microsoft Cloud Partner Program

Figure 9.9 Major cloud vendor programs.

Source: © Sally Ann Frank

Channel partners can be industry-specific as well. For example, integrate .ai set up a partnership with DNAstack. "In partnership with integrate.ai, DNAstack is helping researchers access more data to drive faster discoveries and crack the code on complex disorders."[22] Additionally, AEYE Health, the leader in artificial intelligence-based diagnostics for retinal imaging, and Topcon Screen, a leader in point-of-care diabetic eye exams, announced a partnership to deliver point-of-care screening for diabetic retinopathy that uses AI to produce immediate and accurate results.[23]

Managing the Pipeline

Metrics are incredibly important when evaluating the success of your GTM strategy. As the adage says, if you can't measure it, you can't manage it. In this case, you want to manage the pipeline to understand which elements of your GTM strategy are working and which aren't. To do that you need tools and metrics.

- **CRM** – A customer relationship management system is imperative, especially once you have more than a few opportunities that you are pursuing. As part of the Microsoft for Startups program, participants get licenses for Dynamics CRM. Other options include Hubspot, which does have a free version with limited capabilities, or SugarCRM.

■ **Website analytics** – Top website development tools and platforms can report website traffic, enabling you to understand what pages are most popular and help you uncover why your last blog post didn't get any hits. It can be a treasure trove of actionable data that many startups overlook, seeing their website as a brochure instead of the marketing insight engine that it can be.

Before discussing the metrics, let's go over some pipeline basics. There are several funnel models, but I like this one in Figure 9.10, not just because it's from Microsoft, but also because it shows you how to build a funnel (in this case in Excel, though most CRM tools have the funnel capability built in).

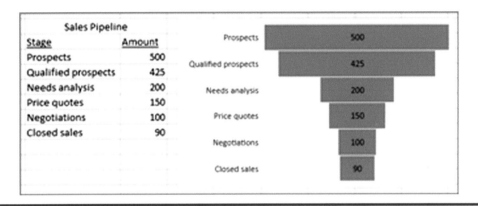

Figure 9.10 **Sales funnel.**

Source: Create a funnel chart – Microsoft Support https://support.microsoft.com/en-us/office/create-a -funnel-chart-ba21bcba-f325-4d9f-93df-97074589a70e.

Before moving on, note that in this fictitious scenario, the funnel begins with 500 prospects with only 90 deals closed. Your mileage will definitely differ. (According to Hubspot, "biotech has an average industry close ratio of 15%. The software industry has one of 22%, and the finance industry has one of 19%."[24] Startup close rates are likely to be lower.)

While the stages vary somewhat depending on the book you read or sales leader you follow, the model above is as good as any. Briefly, they are:

1. **Top of the funnel** – Prospects that could include any of your target personas

2. **Qualified prospects** – Prospects that have expressed some amount of interest through a click on your website, attendance at webinar, or downloading a white paper
3. **Need analysis** – Prospects that have taken an introductory call with you, to share their needs and determine if your solution is a fit
4. **Price quotes** – Prospects that have confirmed your solution fits their needs and are evaluating if it fits their budget
5. **Negotiations** – Prospects are interested in working with you to structure a deal that is more economically sound for them
6. **Closed deals** – Pop the champagne, celebrate the win, publish a win wire (with a blind reference to the customer if they are not willing to let you use their name), and pull the next opportunity through the funnel

In addition to managing the pipeline, there are marketing and sales metrics that you should monitor. There are a wide variety of options, but the ones I find most meaningful are:

■ **Marketing metrics**
   – <u>Impressions</u> – how many people are seeing your social posts
   – <u>Marketing qualified leads</u> – how many people are making themselves known to you, through in-person events, downloading content from your website, clicking on your LinkedIn Smart Links, or any other demand-generating tactic
■ **Sales metrics**
   – <u>Pipeline value</u> – what is the value of the deals in your pipeline
   – <u>Negotiated price</u> – what percentage of the price are you discounting to close deals
   – <u>Close rate</u> – what percentage of opportunities do you actually close
   – <u>Time to close</u> – How long does it take to close a deal; this can also be referred to as opportunity age
   – <u>Cost to close</u> – How much are you spending (marketing, staff, etc.) to win a deal

Taking our model above, we can map the funnel against the metrics in Figure 9.11.

Managing your GTM is key if you want to reach your intended customers. It's both art and science, needing an ability to test frequently, learn quickly, and adapt properly.

Sales pipeline stage	Metric
Prospects	Impressions
Qualified prospects	Marketing qualified leads
Needs analysis	Pipeline value
Price quotes	Pipeline value (updated based on info gathered during needs analysis)
Negotiations	Negotiate price
Close sales	Close rate Time to close Cost to close

Figure 9.11   Funnel stage and metrics.

Source: © Sally Ann Frank

Summary

Pitfall	Best Practice
Improvising your GTM strategy	Build a holistic approach • Keep your target audience at the forefront • Consider partnering with complementary organizations • Monitor metrics and refine strategy accordingly

Resources

- The Proven Process for Developing a Go-to-Market Strategy [+Templates] (hubspot.com).
- Outside In: The Power of Putting Customers at the Center of Your Business: Manning, Harley, Bodine, Kerry, Bernoff, Josh: Amazon.com: Kindle Store: eBook.
- Customer Understanding: Three Ways to Put the "Customer" in Customer Experience (and at the Heart of Your Business): Franz, Annette: 9781686886812: Amazon.com: Books.
- https://ascrs.org/clinical-education/presentations-on-demand/meetings /2023-ascrs-annual-meeting/sessions/2023-microsoft.
- (78) How to Use LinkedIn Sales Navigator [Features, Benefits, and Hacks] | LinkedIn.
- Publish Articles on LinkedIn | LinkedIn Help.

- 22 LinkedIn Sales Navigator Secrets All the Best Prospectors Know (https://blog.hubspot.com/sales/hidden-sales-navigator-features).
- https://www.gartner.com/reviews/market/b2b-marketing-automation -platforms/vendor/hubspot/alternatives.

Notes

1. The Proven Process for Developing a Go-to-Market Strategy [+Templates] (hubspot.com).
2. 12 Things about Product-Market Fit | Andreessen Horowitz (a16z.com).
3. Activ Surgical Leadership | Board of Directors | Advisory Board.
4. Activ Surgical Leadership | Board of Directors | Advisory Board.
5. Private AI | Identify, Redact & Replace PII (private-ai.com).
6. Digital Health; What Do We Mean by Clinical Validation? (tandfonline.com).
7. Interview with Joseph Kvedar, 6 Aug 2023.
8. https://www.ncbi.nlm.nih.gov/pmc/articles/PMC6550273/.
9. https://www.cynerio.com/.
10. Baptist Health North Florida Selects Hyro to Advance Omnichannel AI-Powered Patient & Employee Engagement (prnewswire.com).
11. Baptist Health North Florida Selects Hyro to Advance Omnichannel AI-Powered Patient & Employee Engagement (prnewswire.com).
12. What Is an Early Adopter? A 3-Minute Rundown (hubspot.com).
13. BeeKeeperAI™ Spins Out of UCSF Press Release - BeeKeeperAI, Inc.
14. What Is an Early Adopter? – TechTarget Definition.
15. Healthcare Innovation - The Future of Medicine (vituity.com).
16. Cynerio Harnesses the Power of Generative AI to Revolutionize Healthcare Cybersecurity.
17. SciMar Home Page - SciMar ONE, Inc.
18. Cynerio Collaborates with Microsoft to Provide Enhanced Cybersecurity for Healthcare Industry.
19. Cynerio Collaborates with Microsoft to Provide Enhanced Cybersecurity for Healthcare Industry.
20. UST Strengthens Presence in the Health Tech Sector with Strategic Investment in Israeli SaaS Start-up Well-Beat.
21. UST Strengthens Presence in the Health Tech Sector with Strategic Investment in Israeli SaaS Start-Up Well-Beat.
22. DNAstack Enables Private Machine Learning on Sensitive Genomic and Health Data (integrate.ai).
23. AEYE Health and Topcon Screen Announce Partnership to Enhance Point-of-Care Diabetic Retinopathy Screening with Best-in-Class AI Technology (prnewswire.com).
24. How Close Rates Are Shifting in 2023 [New Data] (hubspot.com).

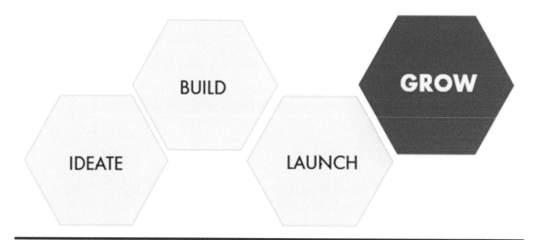

Figure 10.0   Grow.

According to the Oxford Dictionary, growth is defined as "the process of increasing in physical size," "the process of developing or maturing physically, mentally, or spiritually," "something that has grown or is growing," "a tumor or other abnormal formation," "a vineyard or crop of grapes of a specified classification of quality, or a wine from it."[1]

In the medical field, growth is defined as "the progressive development of a living thing, especially the process by which the body reaches its point of complete physical development."[4]

Source: Conversation with Bing, 7/7/2023

(1) https://bing.com/search?q=growth+definition.

(2) Growth | definition of growth by Medical dictionary. https://medical-dictionary.thefreedictionary.com/growth.

(3) https://dictionary.cambridge.org/dictionary/english/growth#:~:text=A%20growth%20is%20also%20tissue%20growing%20on%20the,The%20economy%27s%20growth%20rate%20is%20likely%20to%20slow.. https://dictionary.cambridge.org/dictionary/english/growth.

(4) Growth definition and meaning | Collins English Dictionary. https://www.collinsdictionary.com/dictionary/english/growth.

(5) Growth Definition & Meaning - Merriam-Webster. https://www.merriam-webster.com/dictionary/growth.

Chapter 10

The Growth

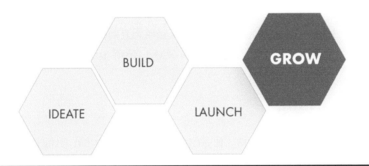

Figure 10.1   Grow.

Source: © Sally Ann Frank

This company is going to take off! We've closed 4 deals.

Years ago, when I was working in healthcare but focused on IoT, I met a company that had a very cool, external, removable heart monitoring device that could be used to monitor patients at home. They had use cases for cardiac patients, elite athletes, and military regiments. It was ground-breaking, had FDA approval, and significant amounts of funding, and they were ready to go big. I remember seeing their product for the first time, and I was enamored with its form and function, as well as the high-quality data it generated. I also remember that interoperability was a concern, as the solution did not yet integrate easily with electronic medical record systems. Another issue was that (at the time) cardiologists were more comfortable with reviewing PDFs of the output, instead of a more dynamic user interface.

DOI: 10.4324/9781032639468-10

The company's GTM strategy lacked focus and consistency, they had no strategic partnerships, and they didn't attend industry events with other leading startups. And yet six years ago, I would have bet on their success.

Today, the only thing that seems to have changed is the team surrounding the founder. Looking back on their development, they were highly innovative in some areas (the device) but lacked the ability to execute in other areas. They also had no significant online presence or brand. While I do hope they succeed in the long term, there are some leading indicators that are not promising. As I write this, on LinkedIn they had one post last week, one a month ago, and another three months ago. Their last blog post on their website was two months ago. These are the typical indicators that a startup isn't reaching its full potential and sparking positive change in healthcare.

Turning a digital health startup into a successful business (or exit) takes a commitment to continual learning, evolution, and growth.

Continual Learning

I spend about an hour each day trying to keep up with this ever-expanding and highly impactful industry, and frankly, it's not enough time. But I try and am disciplined about my learning routine. One of the ways that I stay on top of key topics, trends, and other news is to subscribe to newsletters that email me on a regular basis, some daily, some weekly, and some seem to arrive almost hourly. If you don't keep up, you will be bogged down with so many unread newsletters, that you may abandon keeping up altogether. But it's worth the effort, really. Here are some of my favorites:

- Beckers Healthcare (and they have a variety of newsletters from which to select)
- Axios Vitals
- Morning Consult Health
- Health XL Briefings
- Health IT News

Following thought leaders on LinkedIn or other social channels can be extremely helpful and gives you an opportunity to interact with luminaries in the industry and possibly develop a personal relationship (remember my story about Joe Kvedar in Chapter 6?). My favorite thought leaders include:

■ **Bertalan Meskó, MD, PhD, Director of The Medical Futurist Institute** (https://medicalfuturist.com/) – The Medical Futurist Institute analyzes how science fiction technologies can become reality in medicine and healthcare. As a geek physician with a PhD in genomics, Dr Meskó is an Amazon Top 100 author and also a private professor at Semmelweis Medical School, Budapest, Hungary.[1] He has a newsletter that you can subscribe to through LinkedIn, and Bertalan is prolific, writing about extremely interesting topics that inspire and amaze readers.

■ **John Halamka, MD, MS, President, Mayo Clinic Platform** – For more than 40 years, John D. Halamka, MD, MS, has been dedicated to the technology and policy that enable information exchange among clinical, educational, and administrative stakeholders. Dr Halamka is focused on bringing people together for multidisciplinary collaboration, working across government, academia, and industry to form consortia that accelerate progress in informatics and patient care.[2] Dr Halamka is the author of numerous books on healthcare, and I strongly recommend that you check them out and pick a few to read.

■ **Joseph Kvedar, MD, Professor of Dermatology, Harvard Medical School** (joekvedar.com) – At Mass General Brigham, Dr Joe Kvedar has focused on driving innovation, creating the market, and gaining acceptance for connected health for nearly three decades. He is now applying his expertise, insights, and influence to advancing adoption of telehealth and virtual care technologies at the national level. Dr. Kvedar continues to guide the transformation of healthcare delivery as a respected thought leader, author, and convener. As Editor-in-Chief of NPJ Digital Medicine, a Nature Research journal, he will work to establish the evidence base needed to guide innovation and the implementation of digital health.[3]

■ **Eric Topol, MD** – Dr. Topol is a professor of molecular medicine and the executive vice president of Scripps Research, and the founder and director of its Scripps Research Translational Institute in La Jolla, California. He has published more than 1,300 peer-reviewed articles, with more than 300,000 citations; been elected to the National Academy of Medicine; and is one of the top 10 most cited researchers in medicine. His principal scientific focus has been on the use of genomic and digital data, along with artificial intelligence, to individualize medicine. He is a practicing cardiologist.[4]

▪ **Tom Lawry, Managing Director of Second Century Tech LLC** – Tom Lawry is a strategic advisor to health leaders worldwide and is the best-selling author of Hacking Healthcare – How AI and the Intelligence Revolution Will Reboot an Ailing System. Tom is the Managing Director of Second Century Technology and a former Microsoft executive where he served as National Director of AI for Health and Life Sciences, Director of Worldwide Health, and Director of Organizational Performance for the company's first health incubator. Prior to Microsoft, Tom was a Senior Director at GE Healthcare, the founder of two venture-backed healthcare software companies, and a health system executive.[5]

Another tactic that I use to stay on top of trends in our industry is to set up Google alerts. These alerts enable you to "monitor the web for interesting new content."[6] In the age of ChatGPT, these alerts may become obsolete at some point, but right now, they are tremendously helpful. As someone who works with (versus for) startups, my topics may be different from yours, but here are some of my alert topics, that may also be useful for you:

▪ Healthcare startups
▪ Healthcare and AI
▪ Healthcare funding
▪ Healthcare IoT

I also have alerts set up for the startups that I work with or would like to, and enterprise customers that I also want to monitor. You may also wish to set up alerts for companies you would like to emulate, companies that are competitors, as well as prospects and customers.

This sounds like a lot – and it is. But spending the first 30 minutes each day (with coffee or tea in your mug) reading and learning enables you to be inspired, informed, and ready to face the day.

Continual Networking

Accessing and digesting all this information is just the first step. The second step is to use it to effectively network with people you know and people you don't. By taking extra steps to find relevant articles and other content to post on your social channels, you can set yourself up as a thought leader (not just a re-poster of others' content).

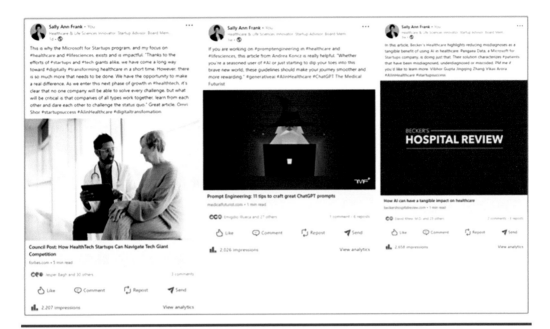

Figure 10.2   Types of social posts.

Source: © Sally Ann Frank

Look at three of my posts in Figure 10.2, one is a soft-sell, one is instructional, and the other is semi-promotional.

- **Soft-sell** – The first features an article from Forbes that I thought was very compelling. Instead of just posting the article, I added my perspective, connecting the topic of the article with my mission at Microsoft for Startups. Pretty simple, but more than 2K people looked. The other thing to note below is that I tagged the author of the article, who is someone I don't know, but would like to. Sometimes, the tagging tactic works and sometimes it doesn't, but it's always worth a try.
- **Instructional** – The second post is sharing information about prompt engineering from The Medical Futurist. While it has little to do with me personally, it's an opportunity to share helpful information about ChatGPT (all the rage at the time of this writing) with my connections and beyond.
- **Semi-promotional** – The third post ties a current trend with one of the startups in my program to promote it to prospective customers. By tying what Pangaea Data does to the trend outlined by Becker's, I'm able to highlight the value of the solution the startup offers, without selling.

The third step is to use the information as touchpoints with people you know and people you may not know, but you are eager to cultivate as prospective partners, customers, advisors, or members of your tribe. For example, I was eager to recruit a particular startup (in your case, it may be recruiting a particular customer) and through my information gathering approaches, I saw an article about the startup. I used the article as an opportunity to show that I'm paying attention and am interested in working with them. You'll also note that the email in Figure 10.3 is brief, to the point, and ends with my goal – to work with them.

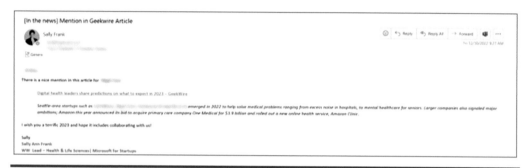

Figure 10.3   Networking with news.

Source: © Sally Ann Frank

In this scenario, the startup founder responded a short time later with an enthusiastic, "thank you," as he had not seen the article, and a promise to get back in touch with me soon about joining the Microsoft for Startups program. Mission accomplished.

This has been an ongoing practice of mine for years, building trust and affinity with key stakeholders across customer and partner organizations. I challenge you to try it five times, and if you don't get at least three positive responses, I will be very surprised.

Networking is one of the most powerful things a founder – or any of us – can do. Nobel Prize winning Israeli-American psychologist Daniel Kahneman found that people would rather do business with a person they like and trust rather than someone they don't, even if that that person is offering a better product at a lower price.[7] That is the power of connection. Be purposeful with your company's brand and your personal brand. Make sure they work well together, and don't send conflicting messages to the marketplace. Above all, be truthful and trustworthy, humble and helpful, and collaborative and creative.

The final strategy to building a constructive network is to identify companies that you want to emulate, companies you would like to collaborate, and companies you compete. Follow them on social media or set up alerts or both, depending on your appetite for information. Make sure that following these companies adds to your knowledge base and informs your startup's strategies. These companies may be other startups, or they may not. For example, Recuro Health is a virtual care startup. They might consider following Teladoc and Amwell, as companies to consider emulating or as possible competitors (or both). Additionally, they might follow Medically Home, a hospital at home company, as a possible partner. Lastly, the companies that you follow will, and should, evolve over time as you refine your strategy.

Continual Evolution

Armed with this influx of targeted information about thought leaders, companies, and the industry as a whole, you set yourself up to continually grow, as a leader and as a company. This chapter began with a story about a promising startup that did not evolve, and we all know what happened to companies (in the US) who were much, much bigger but failed to stay ahead of trends, like Blockbuster and Kodak.

With the expanding adoption of artificial intelligence in healthcare shown in Figure 10.4,[8] many of the startups I work with have been focusing on integrating large language models into the existing solutions, while finding new ways to apply the technology:

■ **Commerce.AI** – A company focused on improving customer contact centers has found a tremendous gap in healthcare that their solution fills and now they are applying generative AI. Andy Pandharikar, CEO and founder of the company recently blogged about their application of large language models for their new product.

auto-MATE™ is a generative AI tool that provides a secure, compliant AI solution for various industries, including healthcare. It ingests unstructured data such as contact center calls, Zoom/Teams meetings or telemedicine recordings to extract structured insights and automates workflows based on those. It offers a library of tasks curated specifically for individual use cases, helping to streamline operations and improve outcomes. auto-MATE™ uses the secure and compliant version of Azure OpenAI model customized by Commerce.AI for industry specific data.

Key Trend 3—Expanding AI Adoption in Healthcare

- AI has been extensively used in workflow efficiency improvement and care delivery enhancements across healthcare systems and will continue to witness expanding applications in healthcare processes.
- Healthcare systems are adopting AI solutions to automate business processes and provide accurate diagnoses and treatment plans.
- AI-based results enhance preventive care, quality of life, and patient outcomes, improving customer satisfaction.
- AI implementation in healthcare drives innovation and creativity and enables organizations to enter new markets with AI-based solutions.

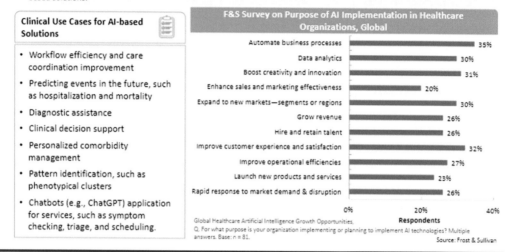

Figure 10.4 Expanding use of AI in healthcare.

Source: Global Digital Health Outlook 2023 (frost.com).

- **Hyro** – This conversational AI company is well on their way to improving their products by using large language models. Their co-founder and CEO, Israel Krush, shares this in a blog post,

  Combining elements of ChatGPT to improve the conversational experience, while opting for a more controlled, and security-heavy engine run on enterprise data, will be the ultimate path forward as we enter this next wave of conversational and generative AI. When up-to-date, specialized knowledge can seamlessly combine with the world's most powerful large language model, the possibilities of conversational automation are truly endless – and Hyro is even further poised to capture the market. Stay tuned, this is only the beginning.[9]

Remember that line in the movie *Glengarry Glen Ross*, "Always be closing"? That's a good mantra for a startup, but let's add innovation to that mantra, because both are needed to be successful as a digital health company in the long run.

This Is Just the Beginning

Healthcare delivery must change, and we need smart, creative innovators like you to help us improve access and quality of care. Avoiding common mistakes, many of which are presented here, will improve your chances of being successful and help us improve outcomes for patients, without suboptimizing any part of the healthcare ecosystem. As you ruminate about the pitfalls and applying some of the best practices outlined here, consider this final question that my friend, startup evangelist and funder Steve Tremitiere shared with me, "What are you kidding yourself about?" This perhaps is the single most compelling question to ask yourself and your founding team. As you build your company, solution, team, GTM, etc., take time to reflect before executing and ask yourself this question. Being mindful of the gaps and where you are kidding yourself is a crucial step to being successful.

Furthermore, continue learning from the journeys of others. In fact, you may want to watch for my next book, *The Unicorn Protocol*, where I share the origin stories and best practices from digital health startups that have thrived and achieved $1B or more in market valuation.

Good luck!

Summary

Pitfall	Best Practice
Failure to continually learn and evolve	Always be ready for change • Monitor technological and ecosystem shifts! • Find leaders to emulate and follow • Network consistently and constructively

Resources

Some of my favorite books on digital health:

- *Unraveled: Prescriptions to Repair a Broken Health Care System*: Weeks, Dr. William B., Weinstein, Dr. James N.: 9781518609251: Amazon.com: Books.

- *The Digital Reconstruction of Healthcare: Transitioning from Brick and Mortar to Virtual Care* (HIMSS Book Series): Cerrato, Paul, Halamka, John: 9780367555979: Amazon.com: Professional & Technical Kindle eBooks.
- *Redefining the Boundaries of Medicine: The High-Tech, High-Touch Path Into the Future*: Cerrato, Paul, Halamka, John: 9798887700403: Amazon.com: Professional & Technical Kindle eBooks.
- *The AI Revolution in Medicine: GPT-4 and Beyond*: Lee, Peter, Goldberg, Carey, Kohane, Isaac: 9780138200138: Amazon.com: Books.
- *Hacking Healthcare*: Lawry, Tom: 9781032260150: Amazon.com: Books.
- *The New Mobile Age: How Technology Will Extend the Healthspan and Optimize the Lifespan*: Kvedar MD, Joseph C., Colman, Carol, Cella, Gina: 9780692906842: Amazon.com: Books.
- Havard Business Review: "Why Startups Fail". (https://hbr.org/2021/05/why-start-ups-fail)

Notes

1. About Dr. Bertalan Meskó – The Medical Futurist.
2. John D. Halamka, M.D., M.S. – Mayo Clinic Faculty Profiles – Mayo Clinic Research.
3. About – Joseph C. Kvedar, MD – Reinventing Healthcare (joekvedar.com).
4. Eric Topol | Medscape Editor in Chief.
5. Hacking Healthcare: Lawry, Tom: 9781032260150: Amazon.com: Books.
6. Google Alerts – Monitor the Web for interesting new content.
7. People Do Business with People They Like and Trust Even If Another Person Is Offering a Better Product at a Lower Price. | LinkedIn.
8. Global Digital Health Outlook 2023 (frost.com).
9. ChatGPT For Enterprise: How Conversational AI Companies Will Leverage Large Language Models (hyro.ai).

Index

A

Academic Medical Center (AMC), 128
Accelerators, 109–110
  basics, 110–111
    access to innovation, 110
    brand cache, 111
    monetization of in-house assets, 110
    monetization of innovation, 111
  completed application, 118
  job posts, 78
  MDSS application, 117
  right for you, 111–113
    application, 116–119
    correct fit, 113–116
Activ Surgical, 86, 124
AI in healthcare, 156
Amazon Web Services (AWS), 38–39
AMC, *see* Academic Medical Center
Angel investor, 51
Artifact, 5, 55
ASEAN, 31
auto-MATE™, 155
AWS, *see* Amazon Web Services

B

Bias, 3
Boasting humbly, 105
Boston Children's Hospital, 123–124
Brand cache, 111
Budget, 6, 45, 111, 144

Build, xv, xvi, 9–10, 16, 18, 45, 47, 50, 53, 64, 72–73, 79, 88, 121, 125, 145, 154
Business model, 87–90
  gap, 16
Buying journey, 6
Buying process, 96–98
  call to action, 102–103
  caveats, 103–106
  CIO/CTO, 97–98
  clinical champion, 97
  committee, 98
  current customers, 99–100
  deck, 98–99
  innovation teams, 98
  offer, 100–101
  pitching to win, 106–107
  procurement, 98
  security leader, 97
Buying roles, 97

C

Cap table, 66–67
Caveats
  boast humbly, 105
  business value, 103–104
  homework, 103
  presentation order, 103
  read the room, 104
  selling your solution, 105–106
Channel partners, 141–142
ChatGPT, 139

Clinician-founders, 95
Commerce.AI, 155
Company, 72–73
  corporate identity, 80
    business model, 87–90
    company name, 80–81
    logo, 81–82
    mission statement, 82–84
    regulatory journey, 90–91
    stealth mode, 91
    tagline, 86
    value proposition, 84–86
    website, 86–87
  name, 81–82
  structure, 73
    team, 73–74
    tribe, 73–74, 79–80
Competition, 140–141
Competitors, 6, 61, 140–141
Confirming, 125–128
  clinical validation, 128
  land and expand, 129
  leverage early adopters programs, 130–133
  pilots, 129
  proof of concepts (POCs), 128
Constructive network, 154–155
Continual evolution, 155–157
  Commerce.AI, 155
  Hyro, 156–157
  use of AI in healthcare, 156
Continual networking, 152–155
  constructive network, 154–155
  continual evolution, 155–157
  instructional, 153
  networking with news, 154
  semi-promotional, 153
  soft-sell, 153
  types of social posts, 152
Corporate identity, 80
  business model, 87–90company name,
    80–81
  logo, 81–82
  mission statement, 82–84
  regulatory journey, 90–91
  stealth mode, 91
  tagline, 86
  value proposition, 84–86

  website, 86–87
Corporate/strategic *vs.* traditional venture
    companies, 52
Correct fit, 113
  confirm cultural fit and stage focus,
    113–114
  evaluate community and alumni
    network, 115
  fine print, 115
  industry alignment, 113
  interview accelerator graduates, 113
  network, 115
  proof of concepts/pilots, 116
  success story, 114–115
  understand their positioning, 115
    JLabs (Johnson & Johnson), 115
    StartUp Health, 115
    Y Combinator, 115
Covid-19, 19, 125
CRM, 142–143
Current customers, 99–100

D

Data, 10–11, 46, 127; *see also* Data privacy;
    Data room
Data privacy, 21–23
  GDPR (Europe), 22–23
  HIPAA (United States), 21–22
  PIPEDA (Canada), 23
Data room, 55–56
  benefits
    due diligence, 55
    internal discipline, 55
  cap table, 66–67
  historical P&L and burn, 67
  investor pitch deck
    ask, 57
    business model, 62
    competitive advantage, 60–61
    competitive analysis, 61
    date progress, 64–66
    financials and metrics, 63–64
    go-to-market plan, 62–63
    investor pitch deck, 56
    management team, 59–60
    problem, 57–59

title page, 56–57
value proposition, 59
making it real, 67–70
SaaS solutions, 55
De novo, 20, 28
Diabetic foot wound boot, 47
DICOM, *see* Digital Imaging and
Communications in Medicine
Digital health, 122
startup steps, xvi
Digital Health Insights, 7
Digital Imaging and Communications in
Medicine (DICOM), 46
Distribution, 141
channel partners, 141–142
DNAstack, 142
systems integrators, 141
DNAstack, 142
Dock Health, 122–123
Due diligence, 55

E

Echo VC, 54
Elements, 13, 56, 122
Elevate Capital, 54
EMA, *see* European Medicines Agency
Emergency use authorization (EUA), 19
Equity, 3, 66–67, 115
EUA, *see* Emergency use authorization
Europe and the UK, 28–29
European Medicines Agency (EMA),
28–29

F

Faro Health, 86
Fast Healthcare Interoperability Resources
(FHIR), 46
Federal Drug Administration (FDA),
19, 24
approved, 27
Class I, 24–27
Class II, 26, 27
Class III, 26, 27
cleared, 27
regulations, 14–15

FHIR, *see* Fast Healthcare Interoperability
Resources
Focus, 6–7, 113, 129, 151
Following up, 138
add value, 138
pick up the phone, 138
Funds, 49–51
data room, 55–70
funding basics
angel investor, 51
corporate/strategic *vs.* traditional
venture companies, 52
lead investor, 51
strategic/corporate investor, 51
venture capital/institutional
investor, 52
funding types, 52–53
Echo VC, 54
Elevate Capital, 54
Global Good Fund, 54–55
Goddess Gaia Ventures, 54
JumpStart Nova, 54
SBIR and STTR, 55
Serena Ventures, 54
WXR Fund, 54
overview of venture capital types, 53
Funnel models, 143
Funnel stage and metrics, 143–145

G

GCP, *see* Google Cloud Platform
General Data Protection Regulation (GDPR),
14, 22–23
Global Good Fund, 54–55
Goddess Gaia Ventures, 54
Going Deeper, 41–43
Google Cloud Platform (GCP), 40
Go-to-market strategies (GTMs), 121–122
competition, 140–141
distribution, 141–142
elements, 122
managing the pipeline, 142–145
production validation, 133–135
product-market fit, 122–124
confirming, 125–133
social media, 139–140

target audience, 135–138
    following up, 138–139
Grow, xvi–xviii, 11, 90, 148; *see also* Growth
Growth, 149–150
    beginning, 157
    continual learning, 150–152
    continual networking, 152–155
    evolution, 155–157
GTMs, *see* Go-to-market strategies

H

HDE, *see* Humanitarian device exemption
Healthcare Information Portability and
        Accountability Act (HIPAA), 21–22
Healthcare system, 1–3, 45–46, 83
Health Insurance Portability and
        Accountability Act (HIPAA), 14
HIPAA, *see* Healthcare Information
        Portability and Accountability Act;
        Health Insurance Portability and
        Accountability Act
Historical P&L and burn, 67
Humanitarian device exemption (HDE), 28
Hyro, 11–12, 60, 61, 76, 105, 129, 140, 156–157

I

Ideate, xv, xxii, 12, 20, 87
Infinadeck, 57–58, 86
Innovation, 7, 98, 123–124, 131–132
    access, 110
    monetization, 111
In-person bespoke events, 136–137
In-person industry events, 135–136
Instructional, 153
Internal discipline, 55
Internet of Things (IoT), 32, 141
Interoperability, 13, 45–47
    Digital Imaging and Communications in
        Medicine (DICOM), 46
    Fast Healthcare Interoperability
        Resources (FHIR), 46
    Trusted Exchange Framework and
        Common Agreement (TEFCA),
        46–47
Interviews, 4–5, 113, 125–127

Investor and customer decks, 99
IoT, *see* Internet of Things
Israel, 31–32

J

JLabs (Johnson & Johnson), 115
JumpStart Nova, 54

L

Launch, xv, 14, 87, 108
Lead investor, 51
LinkedIn marketing campaigns, 138
Logo, 81–82

M

Manufacturing and guidelines and
        regulations (GxP), 34–35
Mapping, 13
Marketecture, 5–6
Marketing and sales metrics, 144
Medical devices, 23–24
    Europe and the UK, 28–29
    Israel, 31–32
    Singapore, 31
    UK, 29–30
    United States, 24–28
Microsoft Azure, 40–41
Minister of Health (MoH), 32
Mission, 11
Mission statement, 82–84
MoH, *see* Minister of Health
Monetization of in-house assets, 110
Monetization of innovation, 111
Moon shots, 125

N

Networking, 136–137, 152
News networking, 154
New technology, 10
    change management, 16–17
    solutions, 16
    trailblazer, 15
Next steps, 101–102, 106

O

Offer, 80, 88, 99–102
Options, 38–39
    AWS, 39
    GCP, 40
    Going Deeper, 41–43
    interoperability, 45–47
    Microsoft Azure, 40–41
    reuse of technology, 47
    systems integrator (SI) partner, 43–45

P

Pangaea Data, 59, 83, 86
PCCP, *see* Predetermined Change Control
        Plans
Personal Information Protection and
        Electronic Documents Act
        (PIPEDA), 23
Personas, 95
    roles, 96
    titles, 95–96
Pilots, 15, 109, 116, 129
PIPEDA, *see* Personal Information Protection
        and Electronic Documents Act
Pipeline management, 142
    CRM, 142–143
    funnel models, 143
    funnel stage and metrics, 143–145
    marketing and sales metrics, 144
    sales funnel, 143
    website analytics, 143
Pitch, 94–95
    buying process, 96–98
    buying roles, 97
    current customers, 100
    investor and customer decks, 99
    next steps, 102
    offer, 101
    personas, 95
        roles, 96
        titles, 95–96
    presentation order, 103
    script, 104
Pitching to win, 106–107

PMA, *see* Premarket approval
Point-solution fatigue, 13
Polls, 4
Predetermined Change Control Plans
        (PCCP), 32
Premarket approval (PMA), 27–28
Premarket notification 510(k), 28
Presentation order, 103
Problem, 1–2, 57–59, 99
    artifact, 5
    bias, 3
    buying journey, 6
    competitors, 6
    equity, 3
    focus, 6
    interviews, 4
    marketecture, 5–6
    polls, 4
    regulations, 3
    research, 4–5
    risk, 3
    security, 3
    statement, 5
    value proposition, 5
Product-market fit
    Activ Surgical, 124
    confirming, 125–128
        clinical validation, 128
        land and expand, 129
        leverage early adopters programs,
            130–133
        pilots, 129
        proof of concepts (POCs), 128
    Covid-19, 125
    digital health, 122
    Dock Health, 122–123
    innovation, 123–124
    moon shots, 125
    RxLightning, 124
Proof points from Hyro, 11–12

R

Read the room, 104
    in-person, 104
    virtually, 104–105

Regulations, 3, 19–21
    change management for medical devices,
        32–33
    data privacy, 21–23
    manufacturing and guidelines and
        regulations (GxP), 34–35
    medical devices, 23–32
    software, 33–34
    UN Map, 24
Regulatory compliance, 14, 20
Regulatory journey, 90–91
Research, 4–5, 15–16, 46, 151
Reuse technology, 47
Right for you, 111–113
    application, 116–119
    correct fit, 113–116
Risk, 3, 27–29, 131
ROI calculators, 140
RxLightning, 124

S

SaaS, *see* Software-as-a-service
Sales funnel, 143
Sales Navigator, 137
SaMD, *see* Software as a Medical Device
SBIR, *see* Small Business Innovation
    Research
SciMar One, 140
Script, 104
Security, 3, 89
Semi-promotional, 153
Serena Ventures, 54
Singapore, 31
Singapore's Health Sciences Authority
    (HSA), 31
Small Business Innovation Research
    (SBIR), 55
Small Business Technology Transfer
    (STTR), 55
Smart onesie, 47
Smart sock, 47
Social media, 139–140
Soft-sell, 153
Software, 33–34

Software as a Medical Device (SaMD),
    33–34
Software-as-a-service (SaaS), 16
Solution, 9
    business model gap, 16
    focus training, 9–10
    using known technology, 11–15
    using new(er) technology, 15–16
    validation, 14
Speed to treatment, 119
Sponsors, 111
Staffing, 38, 111
StartUp Health, 115–116
*StartUp Nation: The Story of Israel's
    Economic Miracle* (Senor and
    Singer), 31
Stealth mode, 91
Strategic/corporate investor, 51
Structure, 73
    team, 73–74
    tribe, 73–74, 79–80
STTR, *see* Small Business Technology
    Transfer
Systems integrators, 141

T

Tagline, 86, 92
Target audience, 135
    following up, 138
        add value, 138
        pick up the phone, 138
    in-person bespoke events, 136–137
    in-person industry events, 135–136
    LinkedIn marketing campaigns, 138
    Sales Navigator, 137
Team, 70, 74–78, 98, 123
Technology, 11–15
    big tech make acquisitions, 44
    change management, 16
    data, 11
    healthcare uses cases, 42
    interoperability, 12–13
    mapping, 12
    mission, 11

options, 38–39
  AWS, 39
  GCP, 40
  Going Deeper, 41–43
  interoperability, 45–47
  Microsoft Azure, 40–41
  reuse of technology, 47
  systems integrator (SI) partner, 43–45
pilots, 15
proof points from Hyro, 12–13
regulatory compliance, 13–14
sales, 2–3
solution validation, 14–15
value, 11
value statement, 11–12
TEFCA, *see* Trusted Exchange Framework
    and Common Agreement
Tribe, 73–74, 79–80
Trusted Exchange Framework and Common
    Agreement (TEFCA), 46–47
Types of social posts, 152

U

UK, 22, 23, 28–30, 110, 127
United States, 2, 14, 21, 24–28, 39, 46, 55,
    79, 90

V

Validation to production, 133, 134
  free, 133
  negotiations, 134–135
  rebates, 134
Value, 11, 122–123
  business, 103–104
  healthcare, 89–90
  proposition, 5, 59, 84–86
  statement, 11
Venture capital/institutional investor, 52

W

Warrior Centric Health (WCH), 106
WCH, *see* Warrior Centric Health
Website, 86–87
Website analytics, 143
Wheelchair cushion, 47
World Health Organization, 1
WXR Fund, 52, 54

Y

Y Combinator, 78, 110, 111, 113, 115, 116